The State of
American Politics

The State of
American Politics

Edited by
Byron E. Shafer

ROWMAN & LITTLEFIELD PUBLISHERS, INC.
Lanham • Boulder • New York • Oxford

ROWMAN & LITTLEFIELD PUBLISHERS, INC.

Published in the United States of America
by Rowman & Littlefield Publishers, Inc.
An Imprint of the Rowman & Littlefield Publishing Group
4720 Boston Way, Lanham, Maryland 20706
www.rowmanlittlefield.com

12 Hid's Copse Road, Cumnor Hill, Oxford OX2 9JJ, England

British Library Cataloguing in Publication Information Available

Library of Congress Cataloging-in-Publication Data

The state of American politics / edited by Byron E. Shafer.
    p.   cm.
    Includes bibliographical references and index.
    ISBN 0-7425-1763-2 (alk. paper)—ISBN 0-7425-1764-0 (pbk. : alk. paper)
    1. United States—Politics and government—2001– .   I. Shafer, Byron E.
JK275 .S73   2002
320.973—dc21   2001048527

Printed in the United States of America

♾ ™ The paper used in this publication meets the minimum requirements of American National Standard for Information Sciences—Permanence of Paper for Printed Library Materials, ANSI/NISO Z39.48–1992.

Contents

Preface

The State of American Politics is an effort to use recent developments in contemporary politics as a route into the main continuing influences that shaped these developments. This means visiting major aspects of modern American politics to look for larger structures and continuing trends. It means revisiting the main events of 2000–2001 to see how they fit into and exemplify—or deviate from—these larger indicators of the ongoing character of American political life.

The elections of 2000 provided an obvious occasion to take stock of the contours of American government and politics more generally. The chapters that attempt to do so were then initially delivered as a series of public lectures at Oxford University in early 2001. In this, the contributors were recruited not just for their expertise in a specific area, but also for their record at bridging the gap between contemporary political commentary and professional political science. Accordingly, they include journalists who pay attention to the scholarly literature on politics, along with political scientists who are concerned to apply the tools of their guild to the explanation of actual current events.

For these purposes, we needed to open with an overview of the interaction between American society and its politics at this point in time. Michael Barone, Senior Writer at *U.S. News & World Report* and long-time editor of *The Almanac of American Politics*, seemed ideally suited to the task. Next, we needed an overview of the policy issues, both economic and cultural, along with the structural influences—social cleavages, partisan intermediaries, and governmental institutions themselves—that connected society and government across the postwar years. This became my specific responsibility.

After that, we needed some focused attention to elite politicking in the modern era, to the character of the interactions and maneuverings of specialized political actors as they attempt to get government—and often, the mass public—to endorse their preferences. James A. Barnes, who covers partisan politics for *National Journal*, seemed again ideally suited for this mission. At the same time, we needed the other side of the coin, some focused attention to the modern character of mass politics. Richard Johnston of the University of British Columbia delivered the actual lecture, though the chapter is a full collaboration with his senior colleagues, Michael G. Hagen and Kathleen Hall Jamieson of the Annenberg Study of the American Electorate, a source of some of the richest relevant evidence ever available.

We then needed to look at the influence of the continuing structure of the three major *institutions* of American national government, namely, the presidency, Congress, and the Supreme Court. Charles O. Jones of the University of Wisconsin at Madison agreed to handle the presidency by taking us from the initial outcome of the election through the transition to a new administration—a distinctively troubled passage in 2000–2001. David R. Mayhew of Yale University addressed issues facing both houses of Congress, with a look at some "deep structures" normally taken for granted, as well as at the *congressional* transition, itself problematic in this reliably eventful year.

Martin M. Shapiro of the University of California at Berkeley introduced the Courts—though they had long since "introduced" themselves, forcefully, into these eventful politics—with an additional emphasis on the way this aspect of the American story typified (or differed from) the court story in the politics of the developed nations generally. Finally, we needed a closing overview—a sort of afterword on the question: Where are we in 2001?—to take stock of all these influences and developments. William Schneider, political correspondent at Cable News Network and author of *The Confidence Gap: Business, Labor, and Government in the Public Mind*, was willing to tackle that tricky task.

Jennifer Knerr, Politics Editor at Rowman & Littlefield, proved responsive to a book proposal growing out of these public lectures, and she has remained supportive throughout. Brigitte Scott, Renée Legatt, and Jehanne Schweitzer then managed the resulting project. We thank them all. Our hope is that readers encounter both a contemporary tour of the main realms of American politics and numerous possibilities for further analysis in what they read. Our hope is also that readers have as much fun engaging these chapters as audiences evidently did in engaging with their speakers.

I

POLITICS AND SOCIETY

1

The Bush Nation and the Gore Nation

Michael Barone, U.S. News & World Report

"**O**ur Queen," said Benjamin Disraeli's character Egremont, "reigns over the greatest nation that has ever existed." "Which nation?" Morley, the Chartist agitator asked, "for she reigns over two." Egremont seemed puzzled. "Yes," Morley went on, "two nations between whom there is no intercourse and no sympathy; who are as ignorant of each other's habits, thoughts, and feelings as if they were dwellers in different zones or inhabitants of different planets; who are formed by a different breeding, are fed by a different food, are ordered by different manners, and are not governed by the same laws." "You speak of?" Egremont asked. The answer, in bold capital letters, "THE RICH AND THE POOR."

That was in *Sybil,* published in 1845, when many Englishmen feared they were on the brink of revolution. But if Disraeli were somehow writing today, about America and not Britain, and if he were looking at the results of the 2000 presidential election, the final answer would be something like THE BUSH NATION AND THE GORE NATION.

These two nations, unlike Disraeli's, are almost exactly equal in number, give or take a few dimpled chads. And this is no coincidence. For American politics has been almost exactly evenly divided for the last half-decade. In 1996, Bill Clinton was reelected with 49 percent of the vote. Republicans held control of the House of Representatives that year with a popular vote of 49 to 48.5 percent. In 1998, Republicans held the House with a vote of 49 to 48 percent. In 2000, George W.

3

Bush and Al Gore each won 48 percent of the vote. And the Republicans held the House once again with a vote of 49 to 48 percent. In three successive presidential and three successive House elections, neither major party has won a majority of the vote.

Nothing like this has happened in American politics since the 1880s—which was also the last decade in which a president won the electoral vote while losing the popular vote and when the Senate was equally divided between the two parties. In the political marketplace in which the two parties strive to maximize their votes, there will be a tendency toward parity of result. But seldom does that tendency produce again and again results as close as these. Something fundamental is going on. Each party has struck a chord, a chord that seems harmonic to one half of the nation and dissonant to the other half. How has this come to happen? And what is likely to happen in the future?

Let me start by showing how this even split between the parties has been summoned into existence over the last decade. Then I shall examine what seems to be at the heart of the division, what factor explains this division as the difference between wealth and poverty explained the division of Disraeli's England of the 1840s. And then I shall try to look forward, to where I think these two Americas may be headed.

THE ROUTE TO EQUAL DIVISION

No strategist of either of the two parties predicted an even division in 2000. Rather, both looked forward, with some plausibility, to their party's winning a national majority in the millennial election. The Republicans looked at the solid majorities for Ronald Reagan and George Bush in the 1980s—they averaged 54 percent to 42 percent—and for Republican House candidates in 1994—52 to 45 percent—and imagined that these would be amalgamated into solid Republican majorities for president and Congress in 2000. Newt Gingrich imagined that he would serve his last of four terms as Speaker as the collaborator of a Republican president.

The Democrats, from the same vantage point of the mid-1990s, looked at Bill Clinton's 60 percent job ratings and at the 50 percent plus showings he made in most polls running up to the 1996 election, along with his even higher ratings during the impeachment crisis, and imagined that they would produce a triumphant majority for president and Congress in 2000. The liberal columnist E. J. Dionne went on to imagine that this Democratic government would be summoned into existence by a majority convinced that government was a useful instrumentality to solve society's problems.

Both sides, it is fair to say, were deeply disappointed by the 2000 results. The Republicans held onto Congress, but by the excruciatingly narrow margins of 222–213 in the House and 51–50 in the Senate. There is no way the Republicans can govern purely on party-line votes. And both sides fought like cats and dogs—I have yet to have a civil conversation about this with my Democratic friends and do not expect to have one any time soon—over the recount in Florida.

How did we come to be an equally divided, 48 to 48 percent nation? We should begin by comparing the 1988 election, in which George Bush (the father) beat Michael Dukakis by 53 to 46 percent, with the 2000 election, in which George W. Bush and Al Gore tied 48 to 48 percent. The Republican percentage went down by 5 percent, the Democratic percentage went up, rounded off, by 2. But these changes were not equally registered across the nation, and this fact is important. There were stark differences between the major metropolitan areas—those with more than two million people—and the rest of the country, two areas that, as it happens, each account for about half the nation's votes. (Major metropolitan areas actually cast 46 percent of the nation's votes in 1988 and 45 percent in 2000.)

On the one hand, in the major metropolitan areas there was a sharp swing to the Democrats. The older George Bush had carried the major metropolitan areas, barely, by a 51 to 48 percent margin. The younger George Bush lost them to Al Gore by a thumping 55 to 41 percent margin. The Democrats gained 7 percent, the Republicans lost 10 percent: this was the work of the Clinton–Gore Democratic presidency. On the other hand, in the rest of the country—the narrow majority of the country—the older George Bush won by 56 to 43 percent and the younger George Bush by a nearly identical 54 to 42 percent. The Republicans lost 2 percent, the Democrats lost 1 percent—not much difference. The Clinton–Gore Democrats, so big an attraction in the major metropolitan areas, were something of a turnoff in the rest of the country.

The result is figure 1.1 showing which candidate carried each of America's 3,141 counties. About five-sixths of the land area of the country is shown in light gray, for George W. Bush. There are only small parts in dark gray, for Al Gore—in the Northeast and on the West Coast, around big central cities, with occasional spots for Indian reservations, fancy mountain resorts, and rural southern counties with black

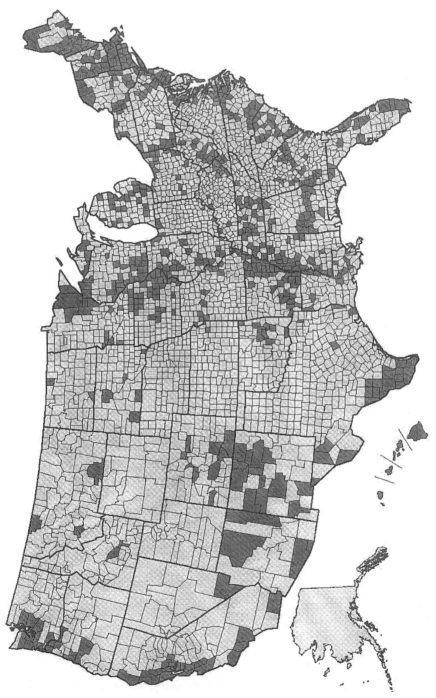

**Figure 1.1 Counties Carried by Bush and Gore
(Light gray: Bush counties; Dark gray: Gore counties)**

Source: Associated Press/ESRI. Data as of November 14, 2000.

majorities. A little less than half the country's population is concentrated in these counties.

Note that this is not at all Disraeli's division between the rich and the poor. The major metropolitan areas that went for Gore are significantly more affluent than the nonmetropolitan areas carried by Bush. Gore carried, overwhelmingly, the Upper East Side of Manhattan and Beverly Hills; Bush carried, overwhelmingly, the coal miners of Appalachia and the farmers of the Great Plains. Gore may have campaigned as the champion of "the people versus the powerful," but the target group of this appeal—the horny-handed workers who supported Franklin D. Roosevelt's New Deal and who can be seen today depicted in the socialist realism murals of the Depression-era Works Progress Administration on post office walls—did not vote for him.

Under Clinton and Gore, the Democrats made big gains in the affluent sprawling suburbs of the biggest metropolitan areas, with their sophisticated, cynical, secular voters, where Clinton's performance got high approval ratings and where his peccadilloes raised few hackles. At the same time, under Clinton and Gore the Republicans made offsetting gains in much of the rest of the nation, with their moralistic, tradition-minded, religious citizens, where voters disapproved of Clinton's conduct and, as importantly, regarded many of his policies as subversive of their way of life.

These responses help to explain the changes in the political map, changes that puzzled so many reporters during the campaign. California and New Jersey, two states easily carried by George Bush (the father) in 1988, were easily carried by Al Gore in 2000—so much so that they were not target states for either side. California is three-quarters metropolitan, New Jersey totally so. West Virginia, so heavily Democratic that since 1932 it had not voted for a Republican except in landslide reelection victories, went for George W. Bush: only five electoral votes, but five votes without which he would not have been elected president. Similarly, Gore's Tennessee and Clinton's Arkansas voted solidly for Bush.

The parade goes on. Iowa, Wisconsin, and Oregon each came within 1 percent of voting for the younger Bush, though they had voted against the older Bush and for Michael Dukakis in 1988. Not much major metropolitan area there. And then there is Florida. In 1988, Florida voted 61 percent for George Bush (the father). In 2000, Florida was the closest state of all, targeted by both candidates throughout the campaign and not decided until December 12. Half of Florida is in major metropolitan areas—the Gold Coast running up from Miami to Palm Beach and the Interstate 4 corridor from Tampa to Orlando.

To voters in some parts of the major metropolitan areas, the choice was as stark and as one-sided as the choice between Lyndon Johnson and Barry Goldwater in 1964. To vote for Johnson was as normal as breathing air; to vote for Goldwater, unthinkable. The same for Gore and Bush. Gore carried Manhattan by 79 to 15 percent and Los Angeles County by 64 to 32 percent—margins of 64 percent and 32 percent, respectively, larger than the 62 percent and 14 percent margins by which Johnson carried Manhattan and Los Angeles County in 1964.

In parts of the other America, the America outside the major metropolitan areas, the choice was as stark and as one-sided as the choice between Richard Nixon and George McGovern in 1972. To vote for Bush was as normal as breathing air; to vote for Gore, unthinkable. Bush carried Wyoming by 41 percent, Idaho by 40 percent, Alaska by 31 percent, North Dakota by 27 percent, Montana by 25 percent, and South Dakota by 23 percent—all margins larger than those by which Nixon carried them in 1972. In the mountain reaches of Kentucky, Tennessee, and West Virginia, Bush carried counties that McGovern actually carried over Nixon twenty-eight years before.

Nationally, the choice was a very close one. Yet in particular parts of the country, places where the metropolitan or nonmetropolitan character was particularly exaggerated, the choice was as one-sided as it was in the greatest landslide victories for both parties in the last half-century. Let me note in passing that this political geography is not peculiar to the presidential race. With some exceptions, it is visible in the results in congressional elections of 1996, 1998, and 2000. It is the synthesis produced by the thesis of Newt Gingrich's Republicanism and the antithesis of Bill Clinton's Democracy.

THE SOURCES OF DIVISION

What divides these two Americas? I look for answers in the Voter News Service exit polls that, if they did not provide accurate projections for Florida, are sufficient for my purpose here. To begin with, these two nations are not separated by generations. Neither candidate carried any age group by more than 4 percent. Nor are they separated very much by sex. There is, to be sure, a gender gap: men voted 53 to 42 percent for Bush, women 54 to 43 percent for Gore. However, married women voted 49 to 48 percent for Bush: this is more of a marriage gap than a gender gap, and hence a clue to what really divides the two nations.

Race, or rather ethnicity, is, as always in America, another divider. Blacks voted for Gore by the near-unanimous margin of 90 to 8 percent and Hispanics, an artificial U.S. Census category, 67 to 31 percent for Gore—although Hispanics in Florida, where their votes were more crucial than anywhere else, voted for Bush. Asians voted 54 to 41 percent for Gore, but that margin came almost entirely in Hawaii; in California, they split 48 to 47 percent. But it is a mistake to regard blacks, Hispanics, and Asians as a bloc of "people of color" that will in time outnumber and outvote whites of European origin. For one thing, whites, as defined here, are still 82 percent of the electorate, and they are anything but homogeneous.

The "people of color" theory is based on the assumption, widespread since the civil rights movement of the 1960s, that Hispanics and Asians will replicate the experiences of blacks. But in fact—and this is the thesis of my forthcoming book *New Americans*—each of today's so-called minorities resembles an immigrant group of a hundred years ago: blacks resemble the Irish, Hispanics resemble the Italians, and Asians resemble the Jews. Today's blacks, like the Irish of one hundred years ago, vote monolithically Democratic and can be expected to do so for some time to come. But they are no longer a growing percentage of the electorate.

Today's Hispanics, like the Italians of one hundred years ago, have different political preferences in different states, depending on the politics of the place they came from and the state they settled in. Currently, Hispanics in California are heavily Democratic because of events in California state politics and because they tend to come from left-leaning parts of Mexico. Hispanics in Texas are much more likely to consider voting Republican because they are from more conservative parts of Mexico and because of the record of George W. Bush. Hispanics in Florida vote Republican because they tend to have roots in Cuba and because they have been warmly embraced by the state's polyglot Republican Party.

Asians, who encounter almost no discrimination at all in America today, except for university racial quotas that deny them places they would otherwise earn, are evenly split between the parties, except in Hawaii, where they are long-settled and heavily Democratic. Their entrepreneurial drive and professional success, combined with the fact that their historic bête noire is not (as it was for Jews) the Russian tsar but the Communist dictator Mao Zedong, suggest that if they are headed toward any party it is Republican.

Or look at income. The political scientists who predicted that Gore would win 56 percent of the two-party vote did so on the basis of formulas derived from the last dozen or so elections that looked primarily or exclusively at economic factors—is the economy growing, and so forth. But man does not vote by bread alone. If the business cycle decided American elections, Gore would have been well ahead in the polls all along. Gore did indeed carry voters with incomes under $30,000 by 55 to 40 percent, and Bush did carry voters with incomes over $75,000—a larger group—by 53 to 44 percent. But these are not large margins in their own right, and they are far lower than in the New Deal period. Indeed, they are far lower than the margins in 1988. Then, Democrats carried the lowest income group by 25 percent; in 2000, by 15 percent. Then, Republicans carried the highest income group by 25 percent; in 2000, by 9 percent.

In other words, neither Gore's championship of "the people versus the powerful" nor Bush's promise of a big tax cut did much of a job in rallying their party's New Deal economic constituencies. One reason, I submit, is that the economic factor that is important in American politics today is not so much income as it is wealth. Voters are not much concerned about temporary drops in income in a country that has suffered only six months of recession in the last seventeen years: low-inflation economic growth has prevailed for 97 percent of the time and has come to seem the norm.

What voters are concerned about is how well they are doing in the lifetime project of accumulating wealth, in residential real estate and, increasingly, in the stock market. George Bush's greatest loss of votes in 1992 came in New Hampshire and southern California, which were also the parts of the nation where housing values dropped most in the 1990–1991 recession. Then, as the stock market boomed after the Republicans won control of Congress in 1994—personal household assets, a good measure of voters' wealth, increased by 8.5 percent a year from 1994 to 1999—the electorate entered a period of great contentment. Low-income voters did not feel in much need of the economic benefits that Democrats promised. High-income voters did not care much about tax rates when they were making vast gains in the market. This increase in wealth helps explain why affluent suburban voters in the major metropolitan areas have shifted away from Republicans: taxes were the one issue that inclined them to be Republican in 1988, and the issue was just much weaker in 2000.

So what is it that divides the two nations? My answer is religion. White voters who identified as members of the religious right—14 per-

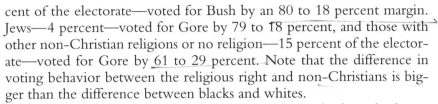

cent of the electorate—voted for Bush by an 80 to 18 percent margin. Jews—4 percent—voted for Gore by 79 to 18 percent, and those with other non-Christian religions or no religion—15 percent of the electorate—voted for Gore by 61 to 29 percent. Note that the difference in voting behavior between the religious right and non-Christians is bigger than the difference between blacks and whites.

These are the fringe groups, however, so let us look at the larger masses. White Protestants—45 percent of the electorate—voted for Bush by 63 to 34 percent. White Catholics—20 percent of the electorate—voted for Bush by 52 to 45 percent, despite the historic preference of Catholics for the Democratic Party. One of the untold stories of the campaign is how the Bush forces worked subtly through little-publicized channels to win over strong, tradition-minded Catholics, obviously with some success. Those who attended religious services weekly or more often—42 percent of the electorate—voted 59 to 39 percent for Bush. Those who attend religious services seldom or never—another 42 percent of the electorate—voted 56 to 39 percent for Gore. The middle group, the 14 percent who said they attended religious services monthly, voted 51 to 46 percent for Gore.

In other words, the two Americas are two nations of different faiths. One is observant, tradition-minded, and moralistic. The other is unobservant, liberation-minded, and relativist. One nation was repelled by Bill Clinton—his frequent lies, his fund-raising scandals, his affair with a White House intern, and his lies under oath in a U.S. District Court. The other nation was charmed by Clinton—his magnetism and fluency, his support of feminism and gay rights, and his closeness to Hollywood figures—or was ready to subordinate any personal distaste to satisfaction with the peace and prosperity plus the steep declines in crime and welfare dependency that occurred during his presidency.

The first nation then saw in Al Gore many of Clinton's deficiencies, the second nation saw in him many of his strengths. So it makes sense that the major metropolitan areas, less observant and more relativist, voted for Gore, and the nonmajor metropolitan majority, observant and moralistic, voted for Bush. Interestingly, the specific issues on which these groups are most deeply divided are issues that were seldom mentioned by either candidate in the campaign, issues on which they were to respond with obvious reluctance in the debates. These are abortion, gun control, and the environment.

Two years ago, Democrats were slavering at the prospect of making these into major issues. That is, they were convinced that abortion, gun control, and the environment would sweep many voters their way. Yet the gains they sought on these issues, had they understood the situation, had in fact already been made. That is, the places where their positions on abortion, gun control, and the environment were popular were by 2000 safely Democratic—California, New Jersey, and the major metropolitan areas. But they were also *un*popular in significant portions of target states—among the large right-to-life movements in Minnesota and Missouri, among hunters in Pennsylvania and Michigan, and among voters who believed Clinton's environmental policies were threatening their livelihood and way of life.

Voters in eastern Washington and Oregon, for example, felt threatened by the proposal to breach dams on the Snake River to protect salmon. Voters in West Virginia and Kentucky felt threatened by restrictions on the use of coal. Voters in the Rocky Mountains felt threatened by land-use policy that fenced off grazing land and protected the grizzly bear. Voters in the Farm Belt felt threatened by the Environmental Protection Agency's proposal to regulate nonpoint-source pollution—which, put in plain English, meant that farmers would have to get an EPA permit every time they used a new fertilizer.

Voters in these states were aggrieved, in other words, by what they saw as a busybody Democratic government that was trying to impose the values of the major metropolitan areas on their local communities, to impose the values of one nation on another. On these issues—abortion, gun control, and the environment—the Clinton–Gore government was practicing, or was seen to be practicing, a kind of cultural imperialism. The Gore nation wanted abortions honored, guns outlawed, and the environment protected by busybody regulators. Meanwhile, the Bush nation believed that abortions are immoral, guns part of a healthy way of life, and the land and water best protected by those who use it every day.

The two nations on these issues have diametrically opposite views of what is decent and moral, just as they have diametrically opposite views on Clinton's personal morality and Gore's assertion that he was under "no controlling authority." They are, on these issues at least, "two nations," in Disraeli's words, "between whom there is no intercourse and no sympathy; who are as ignorant of each other's habits, thoughts, and feelings, as if they were dwellers in different zones or inhabitants of different planets; who are formed by different breeding, are fed by different food, are ordered by different manners, and not governed by the same laws." They are as different as Bill Clinton's preferred vacation spot, Martha's Vineyard, and George W. Bush's hideaway ranch in Crawford, Texas.

GOVERNING ACROSS THE CULTURAL DIVIDE

Can these two nations live together? The historian Robert Wiebe once wrote that Americans could live together because Americans lived separately. In Florida during impeachment, when gun control and abortion were raised as issues, they found themselves no longer separate but living together, uncomfortably. In the peace and prosperity of the late 1990s, they have been mostly content with things as they were and reelected incumbents of both parties at record rates. But when they were forced by the political calendar to choose, between George W. Bush and Al Gore, between a Republican government and a Democratic government, the two nations, almost precisely equal in size, had to face each other and to confront their differences—as much as both candidates and both parties wished to avoid the subject.

George W. Bush now has the opportunity to govern in a way that will extend his party's base as Bill Clinton extended his party's base in the 1990s. Bush starts off with no reliable national majority, but neither did Clinton. There may be an analogy here with the last time the American political balance was so even, in the 1880s. Then, Americans were divided by a central noneconomic issue, the Civil War. But in the 1890s, other issues came along—free silver and hard money, protectionism and imperialism—that shifted the balance.

The key figure was a president seldom remembered today, but often cited by Bush's chief political strategist, Karl Rove. William McKinley was elected and reelected with a bare majority of 51 percent. But he used the new issues to break across the old cultural barriers and establish the working Republican majority that prevailed for the long generation from 1896 to 1930. Rove believes that Bush can do the same.

The cultural divisions will remain. Moreover, abortions and guns will never be outlawed, so that the demands of neither nation will ever be fully satisfied. But the saliency of these issues may decline, and other issues may take their place. There is a common theme to all of the major Bush domestic proposals, on education, Social Security, Medicare, and taxes, that is to provide citizens with more choice and to rely less on centralized authority. When Bush was trailing in the polls in early September, he put up ads that explicitly presented the election as a contest between more choice and more government, and his standing rose.

This is in line, I believe, with the increasingly decentralized character of American society and responsive to the fact that we are, in important ways, two separate nations who live uncomfortably together. As I have argued before, postindustrial America in many ways more closely resembles the decentralized, culturally divided preindustrial America that Alexis de Tocqueville described in *Democracy in America* than it does the industrial America in which my generation grew up, an America that seemed culturally homogeneous and economically and governmentally centralizing. In this view, George W. Bush, though he won fewer votes than Al Gore, is more in line with the grain of American history.

That means, among other things, that the Bush Administration is less likely to practice the kind of cultural imperialism practiced by the Clinton Administration. The Bush nation is less inclined to want to change the Gore nation—indeed, it begins with the despairing notion that it cannot—than it is to want simply to be left alone. The passage of restrictions on abortion, and even the repeal of *Roe v. Wade* by a new Supreme Court majority will leave the current abortion regime in America largely intact: abortions will still be widely available, though there may be a further decline in their number.

We will continue to have the current gun control regime, in which 50 percent of the people live in states that allow law-abiding citizens to carry concealed handguns and 50 percent live in states that do not. Crime, incidentally, has declined more in states with concealed-carry laws; it appears that criminals are deterred if there is a serious possibility that a potential victim may have a handgun. As for the environment, urban-based environmental activists will be unhappy and will prosper from direct-mail campaigns seeking contributions. But Bush policies will reduce the discontent with attempts to change local ways of life.

Bush's proposals for education seem unlikely to invade local autonomy or to impose one nation's values on the other. He seeks greater accountability and testing, and in fact American education has been moving—rapidly in some states, fitfully in others—in the same direction. We will thus get less of centralized bureaucracy trying to impose values from Washington. The Democratic policy followed for the last thirty years—derided by opponents as "pump more money into schools and prevent them from being held accountable for results"—is increasingly regarded as bankrupt and would have been modified even if Gore had won.

Bush's major economic initiatives—on taxes, Social Security, and Medicare—have some potential for increasing support for Republicans in the major metropolitan areas where they lost ground in the 1990s. It may seem odd after what I have said to suggest that economic issues can trump cultural attitudes, but recall that McKinley did not change people's minds about the Civil War; he changed the subject. Affluent suburban voters may not be particularly eager for tax cuts today, but once they get them, they may be wary that the Democrats will raise rates if they get back in—the posture of the tax issue that favored George Bush (the father) in 1988.

As for providing individual investment accounts as part of Social Security, this should appeal most to younger voters who have become accustomed to accumulating wealth by investing in the market. Here is a reform that goes very much with the grain of life in major metropolitan America, and not against the grain in the rest of the country. Similarly on Medicare, the Bush reform may provide the elderly with more choices of medical insurance and replace a system that is centrally directed and therefore inherently unable to keep up with technological and scientific advance. And since the incredibly complex and rigid Medicare regulations currently tend to govern the dispensing of medical care to all patients, a more supple, adaptable Medicare might produce better results for everyone in ways that may become visible over time.

It was conventional wisdom during most of the campaign, at least in Washington as well as in fashionable dinner parties in Manhattan and Beverly Hills, that Al Gore was a genius and George Bush an idiot. My own view is that Bush is a fine political strategist and a good manager, demonstrably superior to Gore on both counts. Gore knew he was going to run for president in 2000 for eight years, and yet he had three campaign managers, four or five campaign strategies, and several abrupt changes in wardrobe. In contrast, Bush hewed to essentially the same strategy throughout, and developed intellectually serious issue positions that served him well in the primaries and in the general election and that, in my view, are well suited to achieving bipartisan majorities in Congress.

He did something else that political scientists predicted was impossible: he beat the much more experienced incumbent vice president in a time of peace and prosperity. He did so by the narrowest of margins, to be sure, and without the fluency of speech to which we have become accustomed during Bill Clinton's presidency. But he earned his chance to build on his 48 percent and try to amass a majority.

Indeed, demography appears to be moving, slowly, his way. Some Republicans look with foreboding at the major metropolitan areas, where they have fallen behind the opposition. Who cares if you make gains in West Virginia when you lose ground in California? But the major metropolitan areas are actually not growing as fast as the rest of the country; they cast a smaller share of the nation's votes in 2000 than in 1988. The 2000 census showed the trend. If the electoral vote had been based on the reapportionment mandated by the 2000 census and announced last month, George W. Bush would have won not 271 electoral votes, but 278. He carried all of the states that gained House seats except California—Arizona, Colorado, Florida, Georgia, Nevada, North Carolina, and Texas—while most of those that lost seats were carried by Gore.

The Americans of the Bush nation tend to have more children than the Americans of the Gore nation, while the communities of the Bush nation tend to welcome growth as the communities of the Gore nation tend to limit it: California's culturally conservative Central Valley is growing faster than the culturally liberal San Francisco Bay area. The fastest-growing parts of the United States are formerly rural counties on the metropolitan fringe, beyond the edge-city office centers, now filling up with family-sized subdivisions, outlet shopping malls, and booming megachurches.

Though many of these are within the boundaries of major metropolitan areas, these counties tend to vote strongly Republican, and with their growth have produced Republican majorities almost large enough to offset the Democratic margins in heavily black or culturally liberal central cities. These are places like Collin County, Texas, 73 to 24 percent for Bush, Forsyth County, Georgia, 78 to 19 percent for Bush, Douglas County, Colorado, 65 to 31 percent for Bush. These "edge counties" are usually ignored by reporters and political scientists, who cannot imagine living in such places, but they are in many ways the cutting edge of America, the wave of the future.

The two Americas face no revolution, like the one Disraeli feared. For the most part, Americans leave plenty of space for their fellow citizens to live as they want. But our politics, in these mostly placid times, will continue to register the angers and the passions that are aroused when one of the nations seems to be threatening to use government to impinge on the other. The prospect ahead is for close elections, closely divided Congresses, bitterly fought battles over issues and nominations—and for the two nations with two different faiths to continue to live together, mostly peaceably, economically productive, militarily powerful, culturally creative, often seeming to be spinning out of control, but ultimately stable, two nations united by the politics that seems to divide us.

2

The Search for a New Center

Byron E. Shafer, University of Wisconsin at Madison

The presidential administration of William Jefferson Clinton bracketed a recognizably new phase of an ongoing political order. That order began with a bang in 1968. This new phase began less dramatically in 1992, with the election of Bill Clinton, as the contours characterizing American politics for the previous quarter-century came under renewed stress. It then ran on to include the election of George W. Bush, son of Clinton's defeated 1992 opponent, in 2000. And it crucially subsumed not just another presidential election, the Clinton reelection of 1996, but also the major legislative events of the intervening eight years. Just as it will surely subsume the main legislative events of the Bush administration, however long that may be.

The distinguishing feature of this new political phase was not an attempt to break new ground, by capturing some great emergent issue for one or the other of the political parties. That sort of change was last seen in its pure form in the 1930s; it was last seen in dilute form in the 1960s. Rather, this new and distinguishing feature was more a strategic attempt to break "old ground." Which is to say: the distinguishing feature of this new political phase was a strategic effort by the successful presidential candidates of *both* parties to find a way to distance themselves from their respective liabilities. Their main motivating goal was thus not innovation but reconstitution: to redress the main drawbacks inherited with their party attachments and thereby allow their existing advantages to register more fully.

It is most common—it is certainly simplest—to talk about such an effort in terms of parties and/or party systems. In these terms, this was an effort, structurally, to rebalance partisan identifications in the general public, as well as an effort, substantively, to move the active party toward the ideological center. Seen the first way, Democrats concentrated on shoring up public attachments forged originally in the1930s, while Republicans concentrated on harvesting a Republican drift recognized initially in the 1960s. Seen the second way, both parties sought to return to the ideological and policy center, in effect modernizing their appeals by adapting them to a changed social world. Seen either way, however—and this is the important point—both notions of how a conscious new political phase arrives are actually more misleading than helpful in understanding the current moment.

Instead, it is necessary to think about the *social coalitions* that underpin policy conflict at any given point in time. And it is necessary to think about the *issue context* that goes with those social coalitions. A focus on *party systems* may still be the most efficient way to gather these two key elements into a coherent whole: parties remain the leading intermediaries to American politics, however strong or weak, reflective or distorting, they may be. Yet a move out to structural influence and policy substance, and within them, to social coalitions and issue contexts most especially, is what is instead necessary to understanding the current moment, "where we are in 2001."

THE OLD ORDER

This bedrock distinction—among social coalitions, issue contexts, and party systems—is central to understanding the current moment precisely because the last of these elements, its party system, continues on from a much older time, shorn increasingly of both the social coalitions and issues contexts that arrived with it. That time was the 1930s. Its issue context was forged by the Great Depression, and secondarily by the world war that followed. Its social divisions were built around social class, though they retained important ethnic, racial, and especially regional twists. Its party system featured new majority and minority parties, a new sun and moon to anchor the tides and seasons of American politics, recasting the roles of the Democratic and Republican Parties, respectively.

The Great Depression initially roiled the partisan waters of American politics without calling forth strategic adaptations capable of institutionalizing a new order. A solid and substantial Republican triumph in the presidential election of 1928 was followed by the Great Market Crash of 1929 and then by equally solid and substantial Democratic gains in the midterm election of 1930. The latter were still mainly a protest against existing conditions, however, rather than an incipient definition of the alternative. Indeed, the presidential election of 1932, won crushingly by the Democrats, contained as many promises of "out-Republicaning the Republicans"—slashing spending and cutting taxes—as it did of major new policy directions.

But from 1933 onward, with the inauguration of the new Roosevelt Administration, the programs that would constitute the "New Deal"—unemployment insurance, old-age pensions, farm-price supports, rural electrification, public works, and on and on—came to acquire a basic social welfare character and brought the welfare state to the American people. Inevitably, the social coalitions that formed up around them acquired a distinctive character as well. These too were initially amorphous, as the vast majority of Americans reacted against unhappy economic and social developments. But as an aggressive welfare state became the clear policy response to these developments, a clear if moderate class division, pitting blue-collar against white-collar Americans, came to be the obvious coalitional result.[1]

The key programmatic divide retained some anomalies, the largest of which was civil rights. In this, an interventionist governmental program on behalf of the less advantaged only indirectly challenged the place of the *Republican* Party as the champion of black Americans and of the Democratic Party as their oppressor. The key coalitional divide retained major anomalies as well, the largest being related to the same programmatic twist. In this, class politics did not realign "the Solid South," because a new social welfare emphasis reinforced the (Democratic) loyalties of less-advantaged (white) Southerners, while a multiclass one-party system—itself reinforcing the civil rights anomaly—reinforced the attachments even of the more-advantaged, so long as the Democrats were so clearly ascendant nationwide.

The political parties that pulled all of this together and linked it up to the institutions of national government were pale counterparts to the historic parties that once gave much stronger definition to a party system.[2] Both drew their strength principally from psychological attachments by individual voters, rather than from organized party machinery. Nevertheless, they did have consequential characteristics of their own. If these were not the great, statewide, patronage "machines" of the late nineteenth century, they did reserve substantial authority to party officeholders, and this reserve allowed party elites to calculate partisan strategy within the overall context in which they found themselves—adding some partially autonomous, further contributions of their own.

For the Democrats, this implied a focus, front and center, on social welfare. It was, after all, the New Deal program that had brought them to majority status; the evident majority of America supported the main planks in that program; and party leaders did not miss this foundational strategic fact. An electoral contest focused on social welfare would return the maximal share of Democrats to office. They could then turn to protecting and extending that economic–welfare program. At the very least, whether legislatively successful or not, they could use the institutions of government to keep policy debate focused on welfare policy.

In the aftermath of World War II and in the face of an exploding Cold War, it seemed equally obvious—it would seem much less obvious thirty years later—that a new international engagement, centered around the containment of communism, would be a major secondary focus. This latter was arguably new to American politics as a whole. A nation that had maintained only a derisory standing army along with a palpable dislike of "entangling alliances" was now being transformed, and the process of transforming it, presumably into a more normal "great power," occupied a great deal of time, energy, and conflict in the immediate postwar years.[3] Moreover, this was not just a struggle internal to the dominant Democratic Party.

Republicans had their own version, and internal Republican conflicts over a response to the Cold War were critical to cementing what was ultimately to become a bipartisan consensus on foreign policy, one destined to last into the 1960s. For a while, the Republican outcome itself was unclear. But the party retained substantial public credibility in foreign affairs and when Dwight Eisenhower used his Republican presidency to solve the problem of its Cold War positioning, that asset would remain available to party leaders in their quest for electoral majorities nationwide. A public priority for foreign affairs could propel a Republican candidate with obvious foreign-policy credentials into office, and he could in turn attempt to use that office to reinforce public attention to foreign affairs.

Yet, the main public priority remained stubbornly elsewhere, on social welfare, so that the main need for Republican Party officials, at least in national contests, was for candidates who could accommodate that dominant issue context. In their successful local contests, Republican Party leaders felt much less need of welfare moderates, and in fact were actively not enamored of them. Yet they needed them nationally in order to be competitive. The party structure retained authority sufficient to address this strategic need. And for more than a generation, the national party found the candidates capable of addressing it: Wendell Willkie in 1940, Thomas Dewey in 1944, Dewey again in 1948, Dwight Eisenhower in 1952, Eisenhower again in 1956, and Richard Nixon in 1960.

Lest these party leaders award themselves too much leeway in deviating from the dominant preference inside their party coalitions, there were also major interest groups affiliated with each of the two major parties, themselves anchored centrally in the dominant issues of their time.[4] For the Democrats, this meant organized labor. The New Deal had revolutionized labor–management relations, and the immediate postwar years were the zenith of organized labor's membership (and political clout) in all of American history. On the one hand, the labor leadership was focused on social welfare policy: on labor–management relations most centrally, but on extension of the welfare state in general. On the other hand, it had no problem with the Cold War consensus, styling itself as the main voice of "free labor" in the world at large.

For the Republicans, this dominant and reinforcing organized interest was actually small business, rather than big business. The times may have been a diagnostic era of corporate growth, perhaps the dominant period of employment in the biggest corporations in all of American history. That did mean serious corporate constituencies in some local areas. It meant serious financial support for national campaigns. It meant occasional "blue ribbon" candidates from the corporate sector. And it meant, most importantly, constituencies, supporters, and candidates who could make their peace with the welfare state. But the bulk of the work of the party was still done in most areas, and especially in more successful areas, by small-business leaders. They accepted the bipartisan Cold War consensus, just as they made sure that the party did not stray too far toward moderation on issues of social welfare.

A NEW ORDER

That composite strategic environment—an issue context, two social coalitions, and a party system—came apart in the 1960s. Yet the ostensible connecting element to this environment, the party system itself, initially continued on. And in that disjunction lay the critical aspect of the new strategic world. There was no obvious single counterpart to the

Great Depression in this successor break. The class basis of opposing social coalitions remained roughly the same. Partisan loyalties in the mass public moved only gradually. Yet the resulting composite was so substantially different after 1968 as to be appropriately dubbed a new political order.

If there was no single counterpart to the Great Depression—and hence no obvious counterpart to the New Deal to follow—there certainly was a large cluster of new issues for the American politics of the 1960s, and hence a new set of policy conflicts for the years afterward. Some of these reduced the force of existing social welfare issues. Civil rights as an emergent issue, for example, while it may in some theoretical sense constitute a subdomain of civil liberties, was perceived by most Americans, white and black, as a subdomain of social welfare—as a request for benefits much more narrowly targeted than those associated with the social insurance programs of the old order.

More of these new issues, however, fell in the realm of what came to be called "social issues" in their time, but which might more appropriately be designated "cultural issues" in ours.[5] Racial rioting, the unhappy face of the civil rights revolution, was part of this cluster. So was widespread campus unrest, the fallout from opposition to the increasingly unpopular Vietnam War. But so, much more lastingly, was criminal justice, crime and punishment, as a core element in a newly emergent issue context. The 1960s saw sharp jumps in all categories of violent crime—murder, robbery, rape, assault—and while racial rioting or campus unrest affected ordinary social life much more comprehensively when it did occur, the spread of crime (and the even greater spread of the *fear* of crime) affected social life much more broadly.

In their immediate time, these issues could all be grouped as concerns about the social order, about the reconstruction (or fraying) of a basic social fabric, pitting an emphasis on personal liberty against an emphasis on social control. Hence the nomenclature of that time, "social issues." But in a longer perspective, and certainly when viewed as part of an issue context that was destined to last, they were probably better seen as an important subdomain of "cultural issues" more generally. Here, the distinction between personal liberty and social control became a larger difference between the protection and extension of individual expression versus the fostering and enforcement of collective norms of behavior.

Cultural "progressives"—the liberals—took the former position, emphasizing rights and liberties. Cultural "traditionalists"—the conservatives—took the latter, emphasizing norms and responsibilities instead.

In the 1960s and 1970s, society provided incentives for the former and incitements to the latter in disproportionate terms, and this imbalance was critical to the partisan impact of these concerns. By the 1990s, a change in this balance would have much to do with their changing impact and hence with the changing phases of a new political order.

The most pointed and dramatic of these incentives or incitements was the rise of a self-conscious (and vociferous) "counterculture" that deliberately attacked traditional norms in the name of the reconstitution of society. Nevertheless, there was a major institutional contribution as well. For this was the time when the U.S. Supreme Court confirmed the shift in its own substantive focus, away from the economic and welfare concerns of the New Deal Era and toward the rights and liberties concerns of what would come to be recognized as the Era of Divided Government. Which is to say: the Court was also extremely important in propelling these same issues (and their same divisions) to the center of partisan politics, through a controversial series of decisions on school prayer, abortion rights, and, once again, criminal justice.[6]

Ironically, the basic social coalitions associated with opposite views on these newly salient issues did not, in principle, have to change at all. The existing division between a white-collar and a blue-collar coalition could, in some abstract sense, have slotted comfortably into a fresh division between cultural progressives and cultural traditionalists. It had long been recognized that the economically wealthier, socially advantaged, and, especially, better educated tended to be more liberal on these cultural issues. Just as it had long been understood that the poorer, disadvantaged, and undereducated were more conservative—this was the basis of those immediate postwar studies that fretted over "working-class authoritarianism."[7]

What kept this otherwise "natural" affinity from becoming merely a new phase in the New Deal Era, an extension of the social coalitions of that era to an expanded issue context, were developments within its party system. In some sense, the disproportionate party of Catholics, the Democrats, should naturally have been antiabortion. The disproportionate party of social traditionalists, the Democrats, should naturally have been profamily. And the disproportionate party of victims, the Democrats, should naturally have been anticrime. Yet changes within the party system, as reinforced by changes in the social and economic composition of society, produced the reverse.

These were not principally changes at the mass base of the party system, in the party identifications of rank-and-file Democrats and Republicans. There was, in truth, a sharp uptick in the share of the public abjuring identification with either party and calling itself independent. But even this was in many ways an artifact of and a response to changes in a different element of the party system. This element was the strategic behavior of party elites. Its change was rooted in *their* policy preferences, and rank-and-file be damned. And those preferences resulted in an exaggerated tension between party activists and their own mass identifiers, a tension that really did become the central aspect of the Era of Divided Government when seen through its social coalitions.

For what motivated those who did the active work of the political parties—and now, in both parties—were principally cultural and not economic issues.[8] Active Democrats became antiwar and thereafter reliably accommodationist in foreign affairs. They became proabortion, as one lead element of being culturally progressive. They hardly became procrime, but they were much more concerned than active Republicans with procedural guarantees for the accused and with constraints on the police. They came to champion dissident minorities on gender issues—first feminists, then homosexuals. Overall, they supported individual liberties over social controls, most especially when the latter were backed up by institutional coercion.

Active Republicans, of course, became the reverse. Moreover, all of this mattered because of a second major change in the American party system. The parties themselves, as organizational machinery, had been in long-term, historic decline, beginning in the late nineteenth century. The coming of the New Deal had reinvigorated individual attachments, both for and against, and this reinvigoration had served to mask the ongoing organizational decay. Yet New Deal programs had ultimately accelerated that decay by making parties less relevant as channels to (and distributors of) the largesse of government. What those parties had retained through the New Deal Era, however skeletal their structure, was a great strategic reserve for party officeholders.

These party officeholders had been recruited by social welfare issues and had been extended in office by the quasi-private character of parties as organizations, so that external challenges were not easy to mount and so that temporally extended work on behalf of the party was the key to gradual progression in party office. This arrangement was critical to extending the issue focus of the New Deal Era, and it was what was finally swept away in the 1960s and 1970s.[9] An increasingly educated citizenry desired to participate in politics—inescapably, still, through political parties—in an individual manner in response to issues of the day. Reforms of party structure in the 1960s and 1970s, again for both parties, provided them the means to do so. The result was political par-

ties that were now networks of issue activists, not machinery dedicated to their own survival.

Not surprisingly, these activists were to be generated essentially by the new *cultural* interest groups, now populating the political landscape. Peace advocates sought out the Democratic Party; military traditionalists sought out the Republican. Abortion activists sought out the Democratic Party; pro-life advocates sought out the Republican. Organized feminists became increasingly consequential and sought a home within the Democratic Party structure; gender traditionalists looked instead to its Republican counterpart. Organized homosexuals looked to the Democrats; supporters of traditional "family values" turned to the Republicans. Gun owners, feeling themselves increasingly under attack, sought a home within the Republican structure; controllers of gun violence looked to the Democrats. The religiously observant, feeling the same threat, looked likewise to the Republicans; organized secularists focused on the Democrats. And on and on.

NEW STRATEGIC IMPLICATIONS

This new division at the elite level was thus critically facilitated by aspects of the party system, especially by a reformed party structure. But it was ultimately underpinned by grand and gross social changes, especially in the class composition of American society, and these had inescapable implications for the social coalitions in American politics. On the one hand, these changes were grand enough to demand some change in their associated political order. On the other hand, they were gross—undifferentiated—enough that they did *not* have specific and pointed implications for the partisan character of that order. Rather, it was their interaction with a changing party system that would determine this crucial applied impact.

As the postwar economic boom rolled across all these years, American society became wealthier, better educated, and, perhaps most especially, more white collar and middle class. Other things remaining equal, this should have meant rising Republican identifications within the New Deal party system from the 1950s onward. Yet as the New Deal Era extended into the postwar years, it was actually the Democratic Party that continued to be numerically dominant. Across the 1950s and into the 1960s, it was another element of demographic change, simple generational replacement—the replacement of pre–New Deal generations with those achieving their political consciousness in the New Deal

Era—that effectively kept the Democrats dominant at the mass public level.[10]

One major, obvious, further implication was that the Democratic Party too became increasingly middle class. One key result was that by the time the new cultural issues could claim a share of a new and dominant issue context, the Democratic Party had a substantial minority within its mass base who were, themselves, actively attracted to these concerns. There was thus a changing issue context for American politics. There was a changing social base for its pursuit. And there was a party system that continued on, in its main rank-and-file outlines, but changed substantially at the elite level, most especially in its strategic potential.

In the New Deal Era, that party system had reserved substantial powers to long-serving party officials to make strategic judgments based on electoral necessities. They were hardly lacking in individual policy preferences, but they were normally accepting of the notion that these could best be maximized through a concern with overall party fortunes. In the Era of Divided Government, that system shifted those powers to party activists energized more directly by policy issues. They too would make strategic judgments. But those judgments were much more likely to be aimed at maximizing returns from the specific issues (increasingly cultural) that had originally recruited them. The result, inevitably, was a new political order, with a new strategic environment.

In terms of the changed character of that strategic environment for American politics, the key point was that there was now a new—and institutionalized—tension between party activists and their own putative rank and file. Which is to say: four key party sectors, not two, now had to be considered in order to make sense of partisan conflict:

- *Democratic activists* were reliably liberal. They remained liberal on social welfare—that did not change—and they added a strident liberalism on cultural values.
- *Democratic mass identifiers*, however, retained a huge body of supporters who remained liberal on social welfare but had never been liberal on cultural values, and they did not become so.
- Likewise, *Republican activists* were reliably conservative. They remained conservative on social welfare—perhaps becoming even more so—and they added conservatism on cultural values.
- By contrast, *Republican mass identifiers* retained a huge body of supporters who also remained conservative on social welfare but had

never been conservative on cultural values, and they too did not become so.[11]

In the longer run, that is, by the time of George W. Bush, these latter individuals—the economically conservative but culturally liberal—being among the best able in all of American society to understand their options and take action in response, were to constitute as much of a problem for Republican strategists as their own internal dissidents would for the Democrats. In the shorter run, however, in the 1960s and 1970s when the Era of Divided Government became established, it was dissident Democrats—those economic liberals but cultural conservatives—who gave an immediate and distinctive changed character to this first phase of the new order.

That order would be consolidated in the 1970s and 1980s, and its strategic problems would be the problem area that Bill Clinton had to address in the 1990s. His arrival, on the other hand, would mark the second distinguishable phase of the new political order, such that the Republicans would, by then, have developed their own version of the same basic (environmental and strategic) problems. Needless to say, when George W. Bush arrived in 2000, he would thus face his own version of the same challenge that had confronted Clinton. The story of their responses, effectively similar responses from Bill Clinton and George W. Bush, is the story of the rest of this chapter.

However, it was the presidential contest of 1968 that kicked off the new era and ultimately gave it its name, though observers at the time could be forgiven for missing both facts. Richard Nixon may not have seemed the most formidable of challengers—defeated for the presidency in 1960, defeated for governor of California in 1962, and forsaking politics dramatically thereafter—but both major issue dimensions of a new political order were to favor his challenge. He was thus to become the bridge to a new political era.[12]

In trying to extend the New Deal Era by pursuing both his Great Society and the war in Vietnam, President Lyndon Johnson had introduced both rising inflation and rising unemployment into the economy, thereby diminishing normal Democratic advantages on the economic–welfare dimension. At the same time, the new cultural issues were to prove even more noteworthy in their impact; they were destined to complete the job of bringing Nixon back to the White House. Racial rioting, campus unrest, and galloping crime contributed, collectively, a major emphasis on public order. And the Democrats, fairly or unfairly, were effectively saddled with the wrong side of all three.

The civil rights revolution was certainly theirs, and if no sane Democrat would have accepted race riots as a logical concomitant, it was much harder for them to disentangle the former from the latter in the public mind. The Vietnam War was certainly theirs—Dwight Eisenhower, in his time, had consciously refused to be drawn in—so that not just a lingeringly unsuccessful war but also widespread student protest against it were inevitably products of their regime as well. Crime did not so obviously "belong" to anyone, but a *referendum* on the rising crime rate could cut in only one direction.

Despite all this, the election was extremely close, so that the result in its time appeared to be simply anomalous. Richard Nixon did narrowly capture the White House but he gained nearly nothing in Congress, being left to face substantial Democratic majorities in both houses. It was only later, in the full glare of hindsight, that this result would come to be recognized as a logical product of the new strategic environment, and hence as diagnostic, not anomalous. "Divided government"—the presidency in the hands of one political party, Congress in the hands of the other—had arrived as an extended fact. The new strategic environment went a long way toward demanding it.

Within this, Hubert Humphrey, the losing Democratic nominee for president, remained a classic embodiment of the Democratic commitment to the welfare state. Some aspects of the Great Society were in disrepute, such as its War on Poverty, but others were to become mainstays of the American welfare commitment, as with Medicare or Head Start, and the main social insurance projects of the welfare state, such as Social Security, were never close to controversial. Accordingly, while the public was more concerned with cultural issues in the election of 1968, especially with foreign affairs and domestic order, it had an easy means of safeguarding its social welfare preferences: it merely returned sitting Democratic members of Congress to office.

THE DEMOCRATS' DILEMMA

Note that this public did not necessarily desire split partisan control of the institutions of national government. It simply had clear preferences on the *two* main substantive dimensions of policy conflict in its time, on social welfare and cultural values. Faced with a party system that would not cater to those preferences—one party liberal on both, the other party conservative on both—it proceeded to choose accordingly. The public would, over time, get consciously comfortable with this initially anomalous partisan outcome, with divided government, but it did not have to desire it actively in order to vote consistently for split partisan control.

Note also that nothing in this pattern implied that the voting public was becoming more conservative on cultural values, more liberal on social welfare. Survey evidence in fact suggests the reverse.[13] From one side, that public was becoming more cautious about adding major programs to the American welfare state, though it would never back away from the main existing lineaments. From the other side, the public was becoming considerably more liberal on cultural values, tolerating a wider array of social behaviors and refusing to tolerate deeds or words that had been far more common when the postwar world began. It was just that the public, at least for 1968, remained well right of the active Democratic Party on cultural values, well left of the active Republican Party on economic welfare.

Richard Nixon—happy to be president, disappointed to remain so far from controlling Congress—actually struggled *against* the strategic contours of a new political era. He continued to emphasize cultural issues, especially traditional values and "law and order," where the Republican Party looked able to expand an existing partisan advantage. But he tried simultaneously to shift the party away from its existing disadvantage on the main lineaments of the welfare state. Thus, he attempted to make his peace with Keynesian management of the economy while accepting a priority for full employment rather than price stability, and to think about Republican ways to pursue popular Democratic programs: block rather than categorical grants for some, tax credits rather than public bureaucracies for others, and formulaic disbursements rather than institutionalized programs for still others.[14]

The Watergate crisis ultimately wrecked any possibility of success for this larger strategic initiative, and Nixon's immediate successors were not even to try. In failing to implement either economic liberalism or cultural conservatism, Nixon's accidental successor, Jimmy Carter, was undone by the larger strategic environment, and left it essentially as he found it. Carter's Republican successor, Ronald Reagan, was to have much more lasting impact. Though what worked for him in the narrow tactical sense, stiffly conservative economics and expanded cultural conservatism, was ultimately to endow the Republicans with their own version of the main Democratic dilemma.

Reagan did successfully best Carter on both major dimensions of ongoing policy conflict, and it was this dual triumph that brought him to office. On cultural values, what he emphasized most in the 1980 campaign was defense and rearmament, and the Iran hostage crisis proved an especially effective foil for those arguments. But what he really did was to concentrate on making the election a referendum on Carter's economic stewardship, from a dramatic energy crisis to galloping stagflation, thereby attempting to defuse any residual Democratic advantage in that domain.

The Reagan reelection of 1984 then reaffirmed, if such affirmation was still necessary, that the main contours of the Era of Divided Government remained solidly in place. When Reagan had secured his surprisingly strong upset of Carter in 1980, he had actually picked up control of the Senate and shaved the Democratic margin in the House. A classic electoral realignment of the sort that had accompanied the New Deal Era, perhaps aborted by Richard Nixon and the Watergate crisis, just might have been under way again. When Reagan was powerfully returned to office in 1984, however, that notion effectively disappeared. He managed to lose seats in both houses of Congress; he would go on to lose the Senate itself in 1986. The initial phase of the Era of Divided Government, born in the election of 1968, was obviously still institutionalized as the election of 1988 approached.

That would provide the context under which his vice president, George Herbert Walker Bush, would try to succeed him. But it was already a context that had generated substantial, ongoing, and heated debate within the *Democratic* Party about how best to address its strategic requirements. Al Gore was to be central to this debate. Clinton would be even more so. The Democratic Leadership Council (DLC) was to be the main vehicle for trying to impose a self-conscious alternative approach for Democratic candidates to the issue context and social coalitions of their era. And the attempt to create—to publicize and to expand—a cadre of "New Democrats" would be at the heart of this.[15]

An early effort to address the national Democratic dilemma in a new political order had been mounted after the 1980 defeat, in the form of the National House Democratic Caucus. Democratic members of Congress were well aware of the problems of an activist-based political party, and members from the South and West possessed "coat-tail" reasons to be concerned about persistent failings at the top of their party's ticket, electoral failings reflecting (in their view) incorrect issue positions for inappropriate social coalitions. But members of Congress collectively were not well placed to shape the national nominating campaign and Congressmen individually would always have higher priorities than reshaping national party strategy.

Moreover, in the aftermath of the Reagan triumph in 1980, many Democrats had still been willing to treat their national problems as happenstance. His substantial reelection in 1984 made that much more difficult, and this time, a new organization with national strategic concerns at its core did result. This was the DLC, which aimed specifically to reposition the national party, with an eye on a majority social coalition. Moreover, this repositioning was to be explicitly and self-consciously centrist. On economic welfare, the DLC argued for more cautious programs with a larger role for the market, while it sought to escape the tax-and-spend and big-government charges of Republicans. On cultural values, the new organization argued for a reinvigorated military with nationalist intentions, and it aimed to put the party visibly back on the side of middle-class family values, while escaping the charge that it was the logical home of the socially deviant and demonstrating that it was not the prisoner of its own organized interests in either the economic or the cultural realm. The Democratic search for a "new center" had effectively begun.

Senator Al Gore of Tennessee carried the New Democratic banner into the nominating contest, though he shared it, that year, with Congressman Richard Gephardt of Missouri, who would ultimately become a leading spokesman for the "Old Democrats." Regardless, it was Michael Dukakis, the governor of Massachusetts, who ended up with the nomination and who was destined, once again, to be undone by the existing political order. It was the defeat of Dukakis that would lead, most directly, to the triumph—temporary, lasting, or transitional—of the self-styled New Democrats.

The 1988 contest was noteworthy among postwar elections for the *absence* of pressing issue concerns on either the economic or cultural dimension. Which is to say: the issue context demanded little, so that the campaigns (and strategic choices) of the nominees mattered as much as they ever would. In this environment, Dukakis did moderate his party's social welfare positions, arguing for fiscal common sense and neutral managerial competence, though he remained an outspoken cultural liberal. Yet because the opposition preferred to play on cultural terrain anyhow, this implicit downgrading of social welfare only played into their strategy. The campaign of the elder George Bush, the vice president under Ronald Reagan, did not miss its opportunity and relentlessly emphasized cultural concerns: defense, the environment, education, and crime, crime, crime.[16]

BACK IN FROM THE COLD?

The outcome was another Democratic defeat. One secondary result was a shuffling of the formal leadership of the DLC, which brought Governor Bill Clinton of Arkansas to the chairmanship of that body. Clinton was already an influential figure in the rethinking of Democratic approaches to public policy, just as he was already a long-shot possibility for the Democratic nomination in 1992. Chairmanship of the DLC would provide him not only with policy support, but also with an initial constituency and, joining the two, with a nationwide organizational network—to introduce the protocandidate around the country and to underpin a nominating effort, if one occurred.

In the event, he did run. He did front New Democratic themes. And he did secure the nomination, though that sequence itself hardly ran in a straight line. Nevertheless, refusing to balance his ticket in the classical fashion, he went on to choose another New Democrat, Al Gore, as his running mate. And he did begin the campaign with explicit New Democratic themes.

> They're a new generation of Democrats, Bill Clinton and Al Gore, and they don't think the way the old Democratic Party did. They've called for an end to welfare as we know it, so welfare can be a second chance, not a way of life. They've sent a strong signal to criminals by supporting the death penalty. And they've rejected the old tax-and-spend politics: Clinton's balanced twelve budgets, and they've proposed a new plan investing in people, detailing 140 billion dollars in spending cuts they'd make right now. Clinton-Gore. For people. For a change.[17]

Be that as it may, the issue context of the campaign itself, that is, the issues of the day as they were forced in from the outside world, would have been equally fortuitous for an Old Democrat. The main issue was the ongoing recession, a major economic downturn. The main subsidiary concern was health care, as unemployment removed many Americans from job-based health insurance and appeared to threaten many more. Moreover, the main cultural concern of the campaign proved to be, not work incentives, resurgent nationalism, or family values, but Clinton's personal character.

That was a world with the orthodox pattern of costs and benefits from the Era of Divided Government: Democrats benefiting from economic issues, Republicans benefiting from cultural concerns. For 1992, however, it was also a world where welfare topped culture in public priorities, and Clinton was narrowly but duly elected.[18] If the new president were to govern as a New Democrat, then, he would obviously have to reassert his priorities *against* an existing environment. Yet because the environment that he was entering, a national legislative environment where the Democrats retained control of both houses of Congress, was one dominated by old elites schooled in the existing programs and organized constituencies of an ongoing party system, the incentives were clearly stacked toward continuity rather than change.

By hindsight, his choices may have been inevitable. The middle-class tax cut was eliminated and a major economic stimulus plan offered instead. Welfare reform was suspended and medical care moved to the number one policy priority—where it then received an Old Democratic solution, the likes of which could probably not have been delivered even during the New Deal Era. Yet the symbolic item that probably made the greatest single contribution to a policy identification for the new administration was "gays in the military," the Clinton attempt to make open homosexuality an acceptable concomitant of military service.

Within one congressional term, indeed, even before the midterm election of 1994, White House strategists had concluded that the resulting combination—stiff economic and cultural liberalism—was a dangerous mistake. Having raised New Democratic expectations, they had been rebranded as an extension of Old Democratic approaches. The response was a serious effort to counteract this perception. There was a determined effort on behalf of free trade, very much New Democratic and putting a Democratic president in active opposition to the largest organized interest in his party: organized labor. And just before election, there was a carefully calculated effort to reposition the party further through an Omnibus Crime Bill, a New Democratic approach to the issue of crime.

That was figuring without the congressional Democratic Party, however. The institutional repository of Old Democratic thinking (and Old Democratic constituencies) responded by converting the Omnibus Crime Bill, so carefully crafted to express New Democratic themes, into a policy albatross. When conservative Republicans demanded a more punitive and less rehabilitative approach, liberal Democrats joined with them to *reject* what they viewed as an unduly punitive and insufficiently rehabilitative proposal. By the time Clinton had secured the compromises necessary to pass legislation, he had been forced to purchase the support of moderate Republicans and liberal Democrats through additional items of divisible spending.[19] The New Democratic themes had largely been lost; what remained was—at least in Republican rhetoric thereafter—the "pork-barrel approach to criminal justice."

The immediate result was devastating. The Republicans seized control of both the Senate and the House, the first time they had done so since 1952, the first time they had done so without a presidential candidate at their head since 1946, and only the third time they had done so *at all* since 1928—three successes in thirty-three attempts. In the short run, the surface drama continued along exactly these lines. A remarkable share of these new Republicans had signed onto a conservative manifesto, the "Contract with America,"[20] militantly conservative on both economic and cultural matters. And their spokesman, Congressman Newt Gingrich of Georgia who became the new Speaker of the House, actually managed to use that document to set the policy agenda for national government for the next two years.

Few successful Republicans doubted, and in truth, many analysts believed, that Republican control of the presidency would follow more or less naturally two years later, creating unified Republican control of national government, to contrast with the unified Democratic control of the opening Clinton years. In the longer run, however, there were two deeper results of this upheaval, results that proved to have more direct strategic impact. In the first, this upheaval forced sitting Democratic President Clinton to return to his New Democratic themes. This approach was to be fully in place by his reelection campaign of 1996, and he would never thereafter deviate in major ways. And in the second deeper result of the 1994 upheaval, the new Republican Congress actually took the Republican Party farther to the right on both major policy dimensions, establishing the issue context that any Republican nominee in 2000 would inevitably have to address.

Clinton did endure a period of obvious strategic uncertainty in the aftermath of the 1994 election, being forced to assert at one point that "the President is relevant here."[21] But in relatively short order, he had not just retreated to economic moderation in its own right, but was effectively able to convert himself into the defender of *existing* social insurance programs, most especially Social Security and Medicare, such that he would be able to run for reelection in 1996 as the champion of those (vastly popular) programs, without having spent anything further on them and without having had to promise to do so.

At the same time, the President, *no longer encumbered by orthodox Democratic elites in control of Congress*, set to work refashioning his own image. What resulted came in essentially the form that had underlain the original proposals for the Omnibus Crime Bill. This time, he actually did welfare reform, not the moderate version that he would have offered in 1993 but the more conservative program—stiffer time limits, greater autonomy for individual states—that resulted from dealing with Republican majorities. By 1996, Bill Clinton would be touting school uniforms, teen curfews, antismoking initiatives, family protection, and police, police, police.[22] Clinton was thus in position to argue that the national Democratic Party had in effect reclaimed the American center.

NEW DEMOCRATS AND OLD REPUBLICANS

The Republican story was by then very different—or rather, it was a different incarnation of the *exact same* underlying dynamic. If years of Democratic success, courtesy of the New Deal Era, had set the stage for a disadvantageous repositioning of the party in the 1960s, especially on cultural matters, years of Republican success in the opening phase of the Era of Divided Government had done precisely the same for the Republicans. For them, however, the impact was still below the surface, in the ability of organized party constituencies to demand increasingly extreme policies, so that the debate over an alternative strategy—a Republican counterpart of the New Democrats—was still to come.

For the Republicans, the Reagan years, otherwise a time of partisan triumph, had seen an important shift in the composition of the cultural dimension, a shift with important incipient consequences. Perceived capabilities on defense and foreign affairs were to remain an asset for Republican candidates throughout the Reagan administration, as they had been since polling first revealed that status in the Eisenhower years. On the other hand, the partisan value of "law and order" as a matter for policy conflict declined, as racial rioting disappeared and the Vietnam War was liquidated. The Reagan administration did make a serious effort on criminal justice, appointing judges who were "tough on crime," but it would always be difficult to secure reliable partisan advantage in a realm where neither side wanted to be the "procrime" party.

Instead, a whole array of even more explicitly cultural issues came to the fore. Reagan emphasized the virtues of religiosity, consistently attacking court policy on the separation of church and state, albeit without much concrete impact. He helped develop the theme of "family values," of support for the traditional family and for the responsibilities that it entailed, that subsequent candidates would emphasize even more strongly. He kept abortion policy—in his case, antiabortion policy, the right to life—at the center of his public persona, and here, there were legislative victories. Government health programs stopped funding abortions where they had previously done so; the United States refused to support international agencies that followed proabortion policies

This shift was powerfully underpinned by a change in social coalitions. If the postwar years had been characterized by the growth of educated, middle-class Democrats who were culturally liberal, those years had also been characterized by the growth of religious evangelicals, the culturally conservative wing of Protestantism generally.[23] This growth went hand in glove with the increasing sophistication of an evangelical ministry, concerned with the moral decay that cultural progressivism represented and skilled at applying new technologies—mass mailing and televangelism—to fight that decay. The 1970s then saw conservative Christianity spinning off explicitly political organizations to help in that fight.

The ideological consistency and social ease with which Ronald Reagan addressed this movement served to bring cultural conservatives into partisan politics on the Republican side. The Reagan reelection of 1984 then both confirmed the place of a plethora of new socially conservative groups in the organized councils of the Republican Party— this was the outcome that analysts trumpeted at the time—and began to confirm their limitations, the outcome that would eventually prove critical to the fortunes of George W. Bush.

But the presence of a growing Republican problem, precisely parallel to that which the Democrats had experienced after 1968, was masked by the electoral success of the elder George Bush against Michael Dukakis. If the Nixon–Reagan era continued unabated, how could there be a problem? Again there was evidence—still precisely parallel evidence to what would become the experience of Bill Clinton—if analysts had wanted to process it. George H. W. Bush did manage to succeed Ronald Reagan in office, but his efforts to loosen the bonds of cultural conservatism that Reagan had bequeathed him proved ineffectual and often harmful.

The elder Bush did offer some educational initiatives in a major policy realm that was open to capture by either of the political parties. Only to see his own congressional party disavow them, so that, if he was to have any fresh educational policy, he actually had to let congressional *Democrats* establish its basic outlines, and then bargain with them over the details. The need to reauthorize the Clean Air Act provided another opportunity to reposition the party culturally on environmental issues. But again, Bush lost the support of his own party and was forced to respond to Democratic initiatives. Even his attempt to address an impending recession, which White House analysts saw clearly by 1990, resulted in attacks from within his own party over abandonment of his pledge of "no new taxes."[24]

Bill Clinton's election might, in principle, have promoted some Republican soul-searching. But within two years, the party had engineered the stunning recapture of Congress. Again, how could there be a problem? And in truth, the main planks of the Contract with America, although most did not become national law even after passage in the House of Representatives, did not actually appear to hurt the party nationwide. All had been carefully poll-tested before being enunciated; most worked as their testing had suggested.

The inescapable turning point (once more in the full glare of hindsight) came instead at the end of the first year of the new Republican Congress, at the end of 1995 and the beginning of 1996, when the new members attempted to move on and fulfill their promise to balance the federal budget. To that end, they needed to control expenditures on the major social insurance programs, especially Social Security and Medicare. And to that end, they shut down the government twice over the Christmas/New Years holidays to force the President to negotiate with them.

They were never to recover. A sign of the potential vulnerability of Bill Clinton for 1996 was the fact that Bob Dole, front-runner for the Republican nomination, had always run close to him and intermittently run ahead in trial heats during 1995. From the period immediately after the second governmental shutdown, on the other hand, their support lines diverged, and Dole was never thereafter a serious threat.[25] Worse yet, being so evidently behind the incumbent president during the nominating season, he was sharply constrained in what he could do, strategically, during the fall campaign.

The Republican Party of 1996, like the Democratic Party of 1992, presented an established—and strong—pattern of constraints on general election strategy. Just as the active Democratic Party was strongly liberal on both economic and cultural issues, the active Republican Party was strongly conservative. Where Bill Clinton worked to relax these positions in the aftermath of the 1994 Republican triumph, however, congressional Republican elites worked, actively and naturally, to extend and institutionalize them. And the specifics of their effort also mattered.

Two dramatic convention speeches at the 1992 Republican National Convention, from the two Pats, Buchanan and Robertson, had put an evident symbolic seal on the party's cultural positioning. The attempts by "Contract" Republicans to balance the budget while restraining social insurance programs had then put an equally evident symbolic seal on the party's economic positioning. And a weak 1996 nominee, Robert Dole of Kansas, Senate Majority Leader, found himself in a serious strategic box. It was actually this box that George W. Bush would inherit and that he would have to try to escape in 2000.

Lacking policy credentials as a serious cultural conservative but having needed the support of culturally conservative activists in order to be nominated, Dole's best available choice on that dimension was to let policy repositioning alone and hope to benefit from the dimension by emphasizing concerns about presidential character. Needing to counter Clinton's obvious advantage on social welfare, just reinforced by the Republican Congress, Dole sought a policy initiative in the economic realm—and came up with a huge tax cut, in the face of a huge budget deficit, despite his own political history as a fiscal moderate with a concern for economic responsibility.

THE REPUBLICANS' DILEMMA

Neither was of much use. Presidential character did remain an issue, and those who gave it priority did vote disproportionately for Dole. But Bill Clinton had otherwise succeeded in putting the cultural values cluster to sleep, neutralizing Democratic disadvantages within it. The economy itself continued to perform robustly, on top of the huge advantages ceded by the Republican Party on basic social insurance programs.[26] And Bob Dole, long a voice for fiscal responsibility within the Republican Party, was only marginally credible as the advocate of a tax cut during a period of economic expansion.

The result was a solid reelection for President Clinton, coupled with the narrow retention of divided government, as Republicans held their substantial advantage in the Senate and marginal edge in the House. The result was also a familiar policy ballet for the remaining term of the Clinton Presidency. The first Congress of this presidency featured continued pursuit of the character issue by congressional Republicans, culminating in impeachment. Just as it featured continued emphasis on social insurance by congressional Democrats, in a crusade to "fix" a Social Security system that actuaries could foresee going into deficit early in the twenty-first century.

The second Congress of this reelected presidency then featured the dispute that no one had foreseen, over how to allocate an actual budget surplus. At bottom, this surplus was a classic product of divided government. The economy had been growing, while Republicans were unable to offer tax cuts and Democrats were unable to offer fresh spending. In any case, Republicans favored large tax cuts, "giving the people their money back." Democrats favored only targeted tax breaks, "extending the prosperity of the 1990s," while addressing some new programmatic needs. Neither side was able to secure its wishes. Deficit reduction became the only alternative.

Both sides, of course, made continuing efforts to take credit for the surplus, with President Clinton achieving a mild edge in the credit-claiming department.[27] If neither side secured their policy wishes, the Democrats again gained a public relations edge more or less by default through paying down the national debt when neither tax cuts nor new programs could be passed. They thus managed to enter the 2000 campaign with almost the ideal partisan scenario: economic prosperity, international peace, and an experienced candidate apparently well suited to their extension.

Enter "compassionate conservatism." The strategic team around Governor George W. Bush of Texas, as he considered whether to run for president in the apparent vacuum of attractive Republican candidates for 2000—whether he could get the nomination and whether it was worth having—was well aware of the national Republican dilemma. In a mirror image of the problems that Bill Clinton had faced (and addressed only under eventual compulsion), the Bush team saw that the Republican Party risked inheriting a public perception as out of the mainstream on social welfare, and now out of the mainstream on cultural values to boot.

They had come a long way from the change of 1968, when it had been the Democratic Party that was evidently out of the mainstream on cultural values, and tottered on the brink on social welfare too. That strategic disaster had been worth a quarter-century of Republican government, unbroken but for the Carter "accidency." Now, however, the Republicans appeared to be even more severely handicapped at the national level. Congress represented a bright spot, a vastly improved situation if still not nearly the one that Democrats had likewise enjoyed until 1994. But the presidency appeared to have lost the middle ground to the New Democrats, to Bill Clinton and then to Al Gore.

> Helping those in need must be at the center of our national agenda. And America's charities, faith-based organizations, and community groups must be at the center of that effort.

> From Philadelphia to Detroit to Los Angeles, these groups are saving and
> changing lives in ways that government has never been able to match. As Pres-
> ident, I will put the federal government on the side of these armies of
> compassion. . . .
>   My Administration will apply conservative ideas and values to the hard and
> persistent issues facing our country. Compassionate conservatism has one great
> goal: to welcome all our people into the full promise of American life.[28]

Compassionate conservatism was to be the gathering concept for a
response, an argument that Republican ways of proceeding could realize the same values dominating the center in American politics. Republicans were not punitive economically; they were not punitive socially.
Indeed, they had programs that were better at realizing common values.
In the process of setting out these claims, they could almost have been
stealing the playbook from the New Democrats in the years leading up
to the Clinton Presidency: "opportunity, responsibility, and community" as the themes and "the importance of work, the need for faith,
and the centrality of family" as their abstract embodiment.[29]

Those themes were, however, blown off course almost immediately
by the nature of the nominating contest. With a bevy of economic and
cultural conservatives to challenge him and potentially chop up his
front-runner status—Steve Forbes, Pat Buchanan, Gary Bauer, Alan
Keyes—Bush needed to move right in order not to be isolated from
the ongoing conservatism of the active Republican Party. When John
McCain instead became his major challenge for the nomination, a mav-
erick candidate appealing to those within the party who were outside
of *its* organized constituencies, Bush was then planted solidly on the
right. By supporting campaign finance reform and *not* appeasing the
religious conservatives, it was McCain who became the default candidate of moderate Republicans.

With moderate Republicans going to McCain, Bush had to have the
solid support of conservatives in order to secure his nomination. There
were further fillips to this strategy, twists along the way that were addi-
tionally unhelpful to the aspiring candidate of compassionate conservatism. Like the fact that the key contest after McCain upset Bush in New
Hampshire arrived in South Carolina, where the active Republican
Party was especially conservative on both major dimensions. Bush tri-
umphed there, and he went on to secure the nomination. But he was
no longer the evident "centrist Republican" that he had set out to be,
the logical counterpart to the "centrist Democrat" that Bill Clinton had
been banged into becoming.[30]

His next opportunity to return to these themes was the Republican National Convention, and he seized upon it with a vengeance. This gathering raised the tightly scripted character of modern televised conventions to perhaps the most extreme point in their history. Yet the script itself was more noteworthy for its deviations. The official party was nearly banished from the podium. Instead of the senators, Congressmen, and governors that the national Republican Party possessed in abundance, there were only "real people," private citizens who embodied some aspect of the Bush approach, whether it be a voluntary organization, a faith-based program, or, most commonly, an educational initiative.[31]

Indeed, the whole "Anglo" party was in short supply. In previous presidential contests, national Republicans had actively flirted with an anti-immigrant and antiminority stance, to help firm up the support of Americans of European family origin. The Bush convention instead featured numerous black spokespersons and an absolute plethora of Hispanics. Some of this was aimed at members of these groups themselves: the Bush team felt that it needed more than a third of the Hispanic vote in order to win an election, and two Texas campaigns had provided substantial experience in seeking it. Strategists were less hopeful about cracking the black vote, but an evident willingness to seek that vote had additional benefits: it signaled to moderate Anglos, as forcefully as anything in their arsenal, that they intended to be policy moderates, not extremists.

It would have been possible, in principle, to do all this in prime (television) time and yet to feature the alternative—party officials and Anglos—in off hours. Instead, it was as if the Bush team was not only sending a national message via television, but was also running a partisan tutorial about the shape of a successful party campaign. The audience for this tutorial was, of course, *the party activists gathered in the hall.* If they went home willing to give the new strategy a try, then that was a major secondary gain from the convention. On the other hand, if the new strategy failed, then it might still be a long time before it got another chance.

BACK IN FROM THE COLD, AGAIN?

The subsequent campaign for the general election, like all general election campaigns, generated peculiar incidents all its own, incidents that the candidate operations had to address quite apart from any overall

strategy. The "rats" advertisements early in this campaign—televised ads
that were argued to have a negative subliminal message embedded
within them—were a particular trial for the Bush operation. The erratic
performance of nominee Gore in the televised debates—changing in
each debate, unsuccessful in all—was a particular trial for their Democratic counterparts.[32] Yet both campaigns did basically follow their strategic intentions for the period from September to November.

In this, the Bush campaign eschewed conventional Republican wisdom, about avoiding social welfare and emphasizing cultural values.
The campaign did use the traditional Republican riposte on social welfare, involving the promise of tax cuts, repeatedly and in a big way. But
it also tackled the question of social insurance programs head on, with
its own plan for "saving" Social Security by providing individual retirement accounts to help individuals structure their own pension programs.[33]

Likewise, the campaign did not shy away from an old stand-by, the
character issue, attempting to tar Al Gore with the sins of Bill Clinton
in geographic areas where the latter was notably unpopular. But it also
made a major effort to acquire "the education issue" for Republicans. A
generalized anxiety about the quality of public education in the United
States—for 2000, this was most often the number one issue in opinion
polls—gave Bush the chance to present himself (as his father had once
done) as "the education president." School vouchers were the more
controversial side of this, national testing standards the less controversial
side, though neither was consensual and both were opposed by the
Democrats.

From the other side, Al Gore retained substantial assets, though most
had strategic liabilities attached. The obvious strategic task for Gore was
to blend New Democratic themes that he had helped pioneer and from
which Bill Clinton had so clearly benefited, with an appeal to the main
organized constituencies of the national Democratic Party, which he, as
a sitting vice president who had done policy business with these organizations for eight years, was uniquely able to attempt. The former would
hold onto the ideological center; the latter would boost turnout among
reliable Democratic votes. Gore pursued both throughout the fall,
accepting the risk that, by doing so, he would fully accomplish neither.

The campaign was also noteworthy for the disappearance of some
ongoing "hot button" concerns, and here, abortion policy is an excel-
lent example. Neither candidate deviated from what had become established party positions: Bush was solidly pro-life, Gore solidly pro-
choice. Both emphasized these positions in the nominating campaign,

and both reiterated them in their acceptance speeches at the national party conventions. Yet the issues then disappeared from general election radar, and it was not hard to see why. Or at least Cable News Network (CNN), which supported its convention coverage with focus group analyses of major speeches, found that a very low point in public attractiveness for the elements of the Bush acceptance speech came with his endorsement of the right to life, just as a very low point in the Gore acceptance speech came with his endorsement of the right to choose![34]

The final result was as ambiguous as such results can be. Al Gore won the popular vote nationwide, very narrowly. George W. Bush won the electoral vote, as narrowly—and about as protractedly—as possible. For Bush, however, even the popular vote was a great improvement over the last two outings. While the electoral vote was, of course, the ultimate improvement. Still, Republicans dropped a small number of seats in the closely balanced House and a large number of seats in the less closely balanced Senate.

Democrats had gone into the campaign believing that they had already found the great American center. Regardless, the American public surely returned to that center: 49 to 48 percent in the presidential vote, 50 percent plus or minus in the electoral vote, 50 percent plus or minus in the Senate, and 51 to 49 percent in the House. But had the Republicans found the center too? And was the result thus a confirmation of a new phase for the Era of Divided Government, in which the initial phase of opposite extremes had been replaced by a subsequent phase of centrist alternatives?

The evolution of Bill Clinton, his policy program and his personal presentation, was warning against any easy early answer. George W. Bush certainly faced the same risky prospect that Clinton had faced, in which a congressional party wedded to the ongoing policy positions of an established order was disinclined to move to any "new centrism." In a perverse sense, the equal party balance that he encountered in Congress could actually be an asset in this regard, making it less apparently possible to govern through a consistent blend of conservative economics and conservative culture.

The Bush team had thought carefully about all this. But then, so had the Clinton team in its time. The new president himself actually appeared more inclined to tack with the partisan environment than to impose a self-consciously new and centrist vision upon it. But then, so had the outgoing president when he arrived in office. The Bush team arrived touting the virtues of bipartisanship, while simultaneously bristling at the preferences of their partisan opponents. The Clinton team had arrived denigrating the virtues of bipartisanship, while simultaneously complaining about the behavior of their opposite numbers.

Major external events could still shape the fate of the new Bush presidency, quite apart from all such calculations. Otherwise, the Bush team could obviously fail by appearing to abandon the compassionate conservatism of the election campaign. Just as it could obviously fail by being deserted by its own partisans in Congress. Both failings did indeed curse the presidency of George Bush Sr. From the other side, the Democrats could only hope to succeed by hamstringing this Bush presidency and retaking both houses of Congress in the 2002 midterm. Just as they could only hope to succeed by avoiding the perception that they were the problem in securing successful governance over the next two years. The outcome, either way, will be major evidence toward the character of a new phase in the ongoing Era of Divided Government—or not.

NOTES

1. Arthur M. Schlesinger Jr., *The Crisis of the Old Order* (Boston: Houghton Mifflin, 1957); and William E. Leuchtenberg, *Franklin D. Roosevelt and the New Deal, 1932–1940* (New York: Harper and Row, 1963).

2. Joel H. Silbey, *The American Political Nation, 1838–1893* (Stanford, Calif.: Stanford University Press, 1991), esp. chs. 1 and 13; James L. Sundquist, *Dynamics of the Party System: Alignment and Realignment of Political Parties in the United States* (Washington, D.C.: Brookings Institution, 1973), esp. chs. 10–12; and Everett C. Ladd Jr., with Charles D. Hadley, *Transformations of the American Party System* (New York: Norton, 1975), esp. pt. 1.

3. David M. Kennedy, *Freedom from Fear: The American People in Depression and War, 1929–1945* (New York: Oxford University Press, 1999); and John Lewis Gaddis, *The United States and the Origins of the Cold War, 1941–1949* (New York: Columbia University Press, 1972).

4. Robert H. Zieger, *American Workers, American Unions, 1920–1985* (Baltimore, Md.: Johns Hopkins University Press, 1986); Nicol C. Rae, *The Rise and Fall of the Liberal Republicans: From 1952 to the Present* (New York: Oxford University Press, 1989); and Byron E. Shafer, "Partisan Elites, 1946–1996," in *Partisan Approaches to Postwar American Politics*, ed. Byron E. Shafer (Chatham, N.J.: Chatham House, 1998).

5. Richard M. Scammon and Ben J. Wattenberg, *The Real Majority* (New York: Coward-McCann, 1970); and James Davison Hunter, *Culture Wars: The Struggle to Define America* (New York: Basic, 1991).

6. Todd Gitlin, *The Sixties: Years of Hope, Days of Rage*, rev. ed. (New York: Bantam, 1993); and Richard L. Pacelle Jr., *The Transformation of the Supreme Court's Agenda* (Boulder, Colo.: Westview, 1991).

7. T. W. Adorno and associates, *The Authoritarian Personality* (New York:

Harper and Row, 1950); and Seymour Martin Lipset, "Working-Class Authoritarianism," in *Political Man: The Social Bases of Politics*, by Seymour Martin Lipset (New York: Doubleday, 1960).

8. Michael Barone, *Our Country: The Shaping of America from Roosevelt to Reagan* (New York: The Free Press, 1990), esp. pt. 4; and William H. Chafe, *The Unfinished Journey: America since World War II*, 2d ed. (Oxford: Oxford University Press, 1991), esp. chs. 12–15.

9. Byron E. Shafer, *Quiet Revolution: The Struggle for the Democratic Party and the Shaping of Post-reform Politics* (New York: Russell Sage Foundation, 1983); Alan J. Ware, *The Breakdown of Democratic Party Organization, 1940–1980* (Oxford: Oxford University Press, 1985); and David R. Mayhew, *Placing Parties in American Politics* (Princeton, N.J.: Princeton University Press, 1986).

10. Byron E. Shafer, "The Two Majorities and the Puzzle of Modern American Politics: Economic Development, Issue Evolution, and Divided Government, 1955–2000," in *Contesting Democracy: Structure and Substance in American Political History, 1775–2000*, ed. Byron E. Shafer and Anthony J. Badger (Lawrence: University Press of Kansas, 2001); and Paul R. Abramson, *Generational Change in American Politics* (Lexington, Va.: D.C. Heath, 1975).

11. Byron E. Shafer and William J. M. Claggett, *The Two Majorities: The Issue Context of Modern American Politics* (Baltimore, Md.: Johns Hopkins University Press, 1995); Everett C. Ladd, "Liberalism Upside Down: The Inversion of the New Deal Order," *Political Science Quarterly* 91 (Winter 1976–1977): 577–600; and Everett C. Ladd and Charles D. Hadley, *Political Parties and Political Issues: Patterns in Differentiation since the New Deal* (Beverly Hills, Calif.: Sage, 1973).

12. Gareth Davies, *From Opportunity to Entitlement: The Transformation and Decline of Great Society Liberalism* (Lawrence: University Press of Kansas, 1996); and Allen J. Matusow, *The Unravelling of America: Liberalism in the 1960s* (New York: Harper and Row, 1984).

13. William G. Mayer, *The Changing American Mind: How and Why American Public Opinion Changed between 1960 and 1988* (Ann Arbor: University of Michigan Press, 1992); and Tom W. Smith, "Liberal and Conservative Trends in the United States since World War II," *Public Opinion Quarterly* 54 (Winter 1990): 479–507.

14. Robert J. Mason, "The New American Majority: The Challenge to Democratic Dominance, 1969–1977," D.Phil., Oxford University, 1998; and Joan Hoff, *Nixon Reconsidered* (New York: Basic, 1994).

15. Kenneth S. Baer, *Reinventing Democrats: The Politics of Liberalism from Reagan to Clinton* (Lawrence: University Press of Kansas, 2000).

16. Jean Bethke Elshtain, "Issues and Themes in the 1988 Campaign," in *The Elections of 1988*, ed. Michael Nelson (Washington, D.C.: Congressional Quarterly Press, 1989); and Jack W. Germond and Jules Witcover, *Whose Broad Stripes and Bright Stars? The Trivial Pursuit of the Presidency* (New York: Warner, 1989).

17. Text of one of the most frequently shown campaign ads from the 1992 campaign. Archived at the Kanter Political Commercial Archive, Center for Political Communication, University of Oklahoma.

18. Gerald M. Pomper, "The Presidential Election," in *The Election of 1992*, ed. Gerald M. Pomper (Chatham, N.J.: Chatham House, 1993); and Paul R. Abram-

son, John H. Aldrich, and David W. Rohde, *Change and Continuity in the 1992 Elections* (Washington, D.C.: Congressional Quarterly Press, 1994).

19. Holly Idelson, "An Era Comes to a Close," *Congressional Quarterly Weekly Report*, 23 December 1995, 3871–3873.

20. Ed Gillspie and Bob Schellas, eds., *Contract with America* (New York: Times, 1994).

21. Press Conference, April 18, 1995, quoted in James W. Ceaser and Andrew E. Busch, *Losing to Win: The 1996 Elections and American Politics* (Lanham, Md.: Rowman and Littlefield, 1997), 42.

22. By 1996, even Hilary Clinton, his First Lady, would be championing social control in a newly published book *It Takes a Village* (New York: Simon and Schuster, 1996).

23. James Davison Hunter, *American Evangelicalism: Conservative Religion and the Quandary of Modernity* (New Brunswick, N.J.: Rutgers University Press, 1983); J. Christopher Soper, *Evangelical Christianity in the United States and Great Britain: Religious Beliefs, Political Choices* (Basingstoke, UK: Macmillan, 1994); and Ralph Reed, *Active Faith: How Christians Are Changing the Soul of American Politics* (New York: The Free Press, 1995).

24. Jill Zuckerman, "Democrats Put up Bill to Meet National Goals Set by Bush," *Congressional Quarterly Weekly Report*, 31 March 1990, 1001–1002; Alyson Pytte, "A Decade's Acrimony Lifted in the Glow of Clean Air," *Congressional Quarterly Weekly Report*, 27 October 1990, 3587–3592; and George Hayer, "Defiant House Rebukes Bush; New Round of Fights Begins," *Congressional Quarterly Weekly Report*, 6 October 1990, 3183–3188.

25. The trend lines are reproduced in Byron E. Shafer, "The American Elections of 1996," *Electoral Studies* 16 (September 1997): 394–403.

26. Ceaser and Busch, *Losing to Win*.

27. "Another Paradigm Shift," *The Economist*, 20 November 1999; and "Budget Making: That Was Then, This Is Now," *National Journal*, 1 January 2000, 24.

28. *Renewing America's Purpose: Policy Addresses of George W. Bush, July 1999–July 2000* (Washington, D.C.: Republican National Committee, 2000), 109.

29. Kenneth S. Baer, "Clinton Held the Center All Along," *Los Angeles Times*, 21 January 2001.

30. James W. Ceaser and Andrew E. Busch, "The Invisible Primary: The Marathon Begins" and "The Party Nominations: The Three-Way Race," in *The Perfect Tie: The True Story of the 2000 Presidential Election*, by James W. Ceaser and Andrew E. Busch (Lanham, Md.: Rowman and Littlefield, 2001).

31. Carl M. Cannon, "Even Pablum Has a Purpose," *National Journal Convention Daily*, 30 July 2000, 1; David Von Drehle, "Reality Check on a Decidedly Positive Day," *Washington Post*, 1 August 2000, A1; and James A. Barnes, "It's All about Leadership," *National Journal Convention Daily*, 5 August 2000, 1.

32. Richard L. Berke, "The Ad Campaign: Democrats See, and Smell, Rats in G.O.P. Ad," *New York Times*, 12 September 2000, A1; and Richard L. Berke, "The Context: Debates Put in Focus Images and Reality," *New York Times*, 19 October 2000, A29.

33. Michael Nelson, ed., *The Elections of 2000* (Washington, D.C.: Congressional

Quarterly Press, 2001); and Gerald M. Pomper, ed., *The Elections of 2000: Reports and Interpretations* (New York: Chatham House, 2001). See also Paul R. Abramson, John H. Aldrich, and David W. Rohde, *Change and Continuity in the 2000 Elections* (Washington, D.C.: Congressional Quarterly Press, forthcoming).

34. CNN Television News, 3 August 2001, and 17 August 2001.

II

ELITE STRATEGISTS AND MASS PUBLICS

3

The Invisible Primary and the Hidden Campaign

James A. Barnes, National Journal

In his political memoir, James A. Farley, chief strategist to Franklin D. Roosevelt in the 1932 and 1936 presidential elections, correctly observed that: "A political campaign is a matter of years—not weeks or months. Long before the public hears the tumult and the shouting, the preliminary 'build up' has been under way, and every step taken during this preparatory period is usually the result of long and painstaking consideration." Forty years later, Arthur Hadley would coin the term "the invisible primary" to describe a more focused version of the same process.

Actually, *The Invisible Primary* was the title of a book he wrote that described the political events and currents of 1975, the year before the election of Jimmy Carter. Back then, most of the media and even many political professionals still paid little attention to the comings and goings of presidential candidates at that point in the election calendar. Remember, that was even before Carter and other White House hopefuls had to face voters in their own party caucuses and presidential primaries, in places like Iowa and New Hampshire, as they sought to become the Democratic and Republican standard-bearers for the fall.

When Hadley was writing, not much had changed from the 1960s when the great chronicler of presidential campaigns, Teddy White, author of the *Making of the President* series, described what it was like to campaign with presidential candidates in New Hampshire. Said White, "There was myself and usually one reporter from the AP, the *Union*

Leader (New Hampshire's biggest newspaper), and maybe the *Boston Globe.* During the last week of the primary, the *New York Times* would split its wallet and dispatch its Boston Bureau chief to come up and have a look around."

White, who died several years ago, would probably be shocked by the scene in New Hampshire today. You may have seen the pictures on CNN of what it is like when these White House hopefuls are trudging through the snows of New Hampshire to greet the voters: they are surrounded by a small army of reporters and television camera crews, making it nearly impossible for the candidate to shake anyone's hand, let alone have an intimate conversation with a voter.

In any case, what Hadley learned is that the events that take place the year before the election, and before the first caucus and primary votes are cast, are critical to understanding the outcome of those ballots. He observed how a little-known, former, one-term governor of Georgia was able to travel around Iowa and New Hampshire and, largely unseen, build a grassroots organization and a personal following that enabled him to win the Iowa caucuses and the New Hampshire primary, launching Carter to the 1976 Democratic presidential nomination and ultimately the presidency.

Not surprisingly, many other candidates have followed the Carter model, with varying degrees of success. Moreover, the length of the invisible primary has grown longer and longer with each passing election. Senator Joe Biden of Delaware, who briefly sought the 1988 Democratic presidential nomination, will travel to New Hampshire next month—March 2001—to address Manchester party loyalists at their traditional St. Patrick's Day fund-raiser. Senator John Edwards of North Carolina, who was on the short list of vice presidential prospects for Al Gore, began after the 2000 election to make himself available for a series of friendly chats with reporters in Washington. Indeed, a few eyebrows were raised when Bill Clinton, visiting New Hampshire in January 2001 for the last time before he left the White House, joked that with the election of his wife in New York, New Hampshire might now have an extra senator to look after the state's interests.

What I would like to do in this chapter is look back at what I think were the critical events and political dynamics of the invisible primary for the 2000 campaign, the ones that shaped the actual outcome of both the Democratic and Republican presidential nominating contests. I shall also try to give you a little backroom flavor of how these campaigns are run.

ELECTION NIGHT 1998

For former vice president Al Gore, you might say that the invisible primary was a seven-year affair. Every vice president knows that that position is the surest route to the Oval Office, and every vice president to some extent begins the tireless process of building political chits and IOUs, maybe helping a constituency group gain access to the administration for a pet proposal, maybe helping a Democratic law maker get financial aide for his district, maybe going out to speak at a state party fund-raiser.

Gore was no slouch in this department. He curried support with public-sector unions by weighing in against New Democrat proposals to allow nonunion welfare service providers. Nearly every time he traveled somewhere, he was announcing some kind of administration initiative that would mean so many dollars to whichever district he happened to be visiting that day. And he was a frequent flyer. Before 2000, he had logged more than fifty trips to California alone as vice president.

Despite these activities, it is fair to say that Gore spent most of his time as Bill Clinton's second-in-command preparing himself to be the best president, as opposed to being the best candidate for the presidency. Nevertheless, on the night of the 1998 midterm elections, the scene at the vice president's official residence was a happy one. With President Clinton embroiled in the Monica Lewinsky scandal, Gore had already become the de facto campaigner in chief for the Democrats in the midterm elections. His efforts were to be rewarded that night, as he juggled phone calls to winning candidates across the country. Not surprisingly, one of the first calls he made was to Democrat Tom Vilsak, the new Democratic governor of Iowa, the site of the first-in-the-nation presidential caucuses.

For Gore, the Democratic success that night was critical. The Democrats had actually gained seats in the House of Representatives, something the party in power in the White House had not accomplished in a midterm election since 1934. Had the results gone otherwise and the Democrats lost seats, Gore would have had a major problem on his hands. At the very least, there would have been plenty of finger-pointing from Democrats on Capitol Hill down Pennsylvania Avenue, and the president and his troubles would have been blamed for the party's defeat.

Gore and his friends who had gathered at his home to watch the returns knew what the party's success that night meant: that it was very unlikely there would be a significant challenge from within the party to

Gore's bid for the Democratic presidential nomination. Indeed, as 1999 unfolded, alternative Democratic leaders, one by one, such as Senator Bob Kerrey of Nebraska, the head of the Democratic Senate Campaign Committee, and Congressman Richard Gephardt of Missouri, the Democratic leader in the House and the favorite of organized labor, announced that they were not running. Although they could legitimately claim a share of credit for Democratic success in the midterm, they also realized the vice president would now be the favorite of party activists and fund-raisers.

And support from the latter was seen as critical, since candidates were expected to raise $20 million in 1999 in order to have sufficient funds to compete in the blizzard of primary contests that were going to be held in 2000, on the first Tuesday in March. Even the sex scandal that had engulfed the White House was now working to Gore's advantage. Because Republicans were so aggressive in pushing impeachment, the Democrats in Congress, flush with their success in the midterm elections, were rallying around Clinton and attacking the Republicans as extremists. As one senior adviser to House leader Gephardt moaned to me at the time, any attack on Gore would be seen as an attack on Clinton, who was still popular with the party rank and file. "How could you run against him?"

Only Bill Bradley, a former Democratic senator from New Jersey and something of a party outsider, threw his hat in the ring. With that lone (if consequential) exception, the winnowing of the Democratic presidential field that normally takes place after the Iowa caucuses and the New Hampshire primary proved to be essentially complete by election night 1998.

There was only one sour note that evening for the vice president. In the national survey of voters as they left the polling both, they were asked whom they preferred for president in a hypothetical contest in 2000, Vice President Gore or George W. Bush, the Republican governor of Texas. By a 51 to 39 percent margin, the voters favored Bush.

Down in Austin that night, George W. Bush was in an upbeat mood too. He had not spent nearly as much time out of the state campaigning for Republicans as the vice president had for Democrats, but Bush had won reelection with more than two-thirds of the vote. He told his supporters gathered at hotel not too far from the state capitol that his own sweeping victory was an endorsement of his philosophy and policies, which were both conservative and compassionate. At his victory party, the governor saw his close friend, Brad Freeman, an investment banker from Los Angeles, who was a key California fund-raiser for Bush, and invited him back to the governor's mansion to spend the night. Freeman told me that Bush would not say that he would seek the presidency that night, but that he knew that decision lay before him.

When he sought reelection in 1998, Bush, the son of the former president, maintained that he was giving no thought to the idea of running for president. But Bush's top political aides were certainly giving thought to the proposition, and in April and early May of that year, they met in secret, first in Austin and then again at the Dallas airport, to prepare for a campaign, just in case. At the end of the May, however, Don Evans, Bush's long-time friend and past and present finance chairman for his campaigns, called a halt to these meetings. Bush had not attended any, though of course he was aware of them. But he was also nervous that if their existence leaked out to the press, it would complicate his ability to maintain that the only thing on his mind was reelection as governor of Texas.

Yet a few lasting things came out of that final meeting. One was the guess that the South Carolina primary would be the pivotal contest in the Republican presidential nominating struggle, and that Bush would have to win it at all costs. By contrast, and even at that early date, there was nervousness about how well a southern Republican like Bush would play with the quirky and idiosyncratic voters of New Hampshire. In time, both of these determinations would prove well founded.

At the time, Bush was emerging as a strong contender for the Republican presidential nomination, indeed the favorite of the party rank and file, a phenomenon that puzzled the governor's advisers. "I'm mystified, and so are the rest of us," Bush's pollster, Fred Steeper, told me at the time. "He's not on the evening news." To try to get hold of what was going on, Steeper conducted a poll. Some of the verbatims, the open-ended responses of the people surveyed by Steeper when they were asked about Bush, suggested substantial (albeit beneficial) confusion:

"I don't think he did that bad a job the first time around."

"He handled the problem in the Persian Gulf well."

Obviously, some of the respondents thought the former president was planning a comeback. But most of the comments were more along these lines:

"If he has his father's values, I'll vote for him."

In January 1998, according to a *Wall Street Journal*/NBC News poll, Bush was the favorite of 26 percent of Republicans for the party's presidential nomination. By December of that year, he would be the nomination favorite of 52 percent of the Republicans surveyed by the *Journal* and NBC News. Other polls showed similar growth in Bush's support among Republicans, which increased slowly but surely throughout the year.

How did the governor of Texas, who had barely set foot outside the state in 1998 and done little specifically to raise his profile, double his standing over the rest of the Republican field? Note that other surveys showed similar results. But what had happened?

Monica Lewinsky happened. As the Lewinsky scandal was rallying Democrats to their leader, it was causing Republicans to coalesce around Bush in 1998. From one side, Republicans were looking at Lewinsky and remembering *President* Bush. While George H. W. Bush had had his flaws, he was widely perceived to be an individual of integrity, probity, and stability. From the other side, his fellow governors—fellow governors of the son, George W. Bush—already liked him and wanted one of their own, not a member of the discredited Republican leadership in Congress, to head the ticket in 2000. All thirty-two Republican governors ultimately endorsed Bush's nomination, while when Bush's father had sought (and won) the 1988 Republican nomination, only ten had supported him.

For George W. Bush, that meant that he could count on the support of most local party workers and activists who owed their allegiance to a Republican governor. He went on to collect the endorsements of other party elected officials with much the same gusto. But it was to be the consolidation of financial support within the party that was the critical addition to Bush's ultimate success. He was to garner such widespread backing from Republican fund-raisers that in the first month of his active campaign, March 1999, he raised $7 million. By the end of the first half of the year, he had collected an astounding $36 million. That was more money than Bob Dole had raised in all of 1995 and 1996 for his nominating campaign.

With this kind of early financial support, Bush and his advisers knew that he would be able to forgo federal matching funds, major public money that candidates for presidential nominations can qualify for. As a result, he would be able to escape any limits on campaign spending, nationally and in the individual states. Most of his rivals had to abide by these limits because they could not raise enough money without the federal matching funds to wage a viable campaign. What that meant was that Bush would be able to outspend all of his opponents, except for magazine publisher Steve Forbes who was self-financing his campaign with his own personal fortune.

THE INVISIBLE PRIMARY UNFOLDS

However, in early 1999, Bush was not the only Republican candidate stirring. John McCain, a senator from Arizona, was interested in entering the fray, and his pollster, Bill McInturff, conducted some focus groups—a small gathering of about a dozen or so voters who are interviewed in depth about an issue or a candidate—to ascertain McCain's potential.

First, McInturff showed his focus groups a set of two-minute video clips of the likely Republican presidential candidates, talking from one of their standard stump speeches. The participants were holding little boxes with dials on them. If they liked what they heard, they would turn the dial to the right; if they did not care for what they heard, they could keep the dial fixed or perhaps turn it to the left. McInturff said that McCain's excerpt tested well in comparison to his potential rival's.

Then, McInturff showed the group a six-minute excerpt of an upcoming television biography on McCain, which naturally contained video of McCain's military service and references to the five-and-a-half years that the U.S. Navy pilot had spent in a prisoner of war camp in North Vietnam. After that, McInturff showed the group excerpts of McCain delivering segments of what was to be his presidential announcement speech in April. After they had finished watching and listening to this segment, McInturff asked his focus group members what they thought about McCain and what he had to say.

McInturff told me that almost every man and woman in the group said something like this: "If he [McCain] says he'll stand up to special interests, I believe him. If he says he'll cut taxes, he will. If he survived as a POW in North Vietnam, he can handle Congress." McInturff was of course pleased with the results, but he was also cautious. He had been one of the pollsters for Dole in 1996, a man who also had a very compelling personal story about sacrifice on the field of battle in World War II. But while Dole's personal story was appealing to voters, it did not have a transforming affect on how people viewed the veteran senator, who was a capable congressional leader but still pretty much just a typical Washington politician.

The military conflict in Kosovo then intervened to prevent McCain from formally announcing that he was running for president in April. But this complication to his campaign timetable ended up giving his candidacy a great lift. McCain had some reservations about how President Clinton had handled the Balkan crisis, but when he introduced U.S. forces into the region, McCain backed the decision. That stood in stark contrast to many of his party's leaders in Congress and to most of McCain's rivals for the Republican presidential nomination, including Bush, who were hesitant about backing Clinton's move or opposed it altogether.

Ultimately, McCain would have some problems with the way Clinton was conducting the war by limiting the targets of air strikes and holding back on sending in ground troops. But McCain's initial support for Clinton gained him a great deal of media attention and showed that when it came to foreign policy, he was ready to lead and put partisan considerations aside.

Another key phase of the McCain campaign during the invisible primary occurred in the fall, when the senator went on a book tour. He had been urged for years to write a biography but had resisted. Then, sometime not long after the 1996 election, an enterprising book editor suggested that he write a book about his father and grandfather, both decorated admirals in the U.S. Navy. The editor knew that once McCain was writing about his family, he would naturally include his own life story and his stay in the "Hanoi Hilton."

It is hard to determine just how much the writing of the book fit into McCain's conscious strategy for seeking the White House. I am told that the two are unrelated, but I do not know if I believe that. In any event, the book was definitely not a typical campaign biography. It quickly gained a spot on the *New York Times* bestseller list, rising as high as number three or four. But more important than the book's success was the success of the book tour. McCain traveled around the country and received substantial press attention as he talked about his book and his story in a context outside of a typical campaign swing.

The coverage of the book gave further attention and credibility to McCain's biography, which was central to his presidential campaign. However much the book may not have been part of McCain's grand plan to run for the White House, the book tour certainly was, and his campaign advisers carefully timed the formal announcement of his presidential candidacy to dovetail with the tour. The tour also gave McCain attention at a critical time in the invisible primary, that stage when some of the voters in Iowa and New Hampshire were just beginning to tune into the campaign.

Just as important, though, was the impact that the tour apparently had on the candidate. Several of McCain's advisers report that as he saw the reaction that people were having to him and his book, standing in line for hours for his autograph, McCain gained more confidence that maybe, just maybe, he would be able to connect with voters in a unique way. And it is an axiom of politics that the more confident the candidate is, the better campaigner he or she will be.

In addition, while John McCain was getting ready for his book tour, he spent some time campaigning in California and hit on the novel idea of taking a bus tour through part of the state, on a vehicle that he dubbed the "Straight Talk Express." By that time, McCain had already established his reputation with reporters for being an unusually frank and candid candidate. Which, by the way, reporters love. The Straight Talk Express bus trips would become the signature of the campaign in 2000, reinforcing his image as an atypical politician.

In the presidential nominating contest among Republicans in 2000, Governor Bush was to be the candidate of the party establishment. There was then room for one antiestablishment candidate in the race, as in every nominating contest. Based on the course of events in the invisible primary, John McCain was to emerge to claim the role of the insurgent politician. One other key decision that the McCain camp made early in the invisible primary was to announce that he would not compete in the Iowa caucuses in January 2000. This allowed him to skip the Iowa straw poll in August 1999, an event that would end up as the killing field for many of the Republican hopefuls.

As a way to raise money for their state party, Iowa Republicans customarily hold a straw poll in late summer or early fall in the year before the caucuses. The challenge for all the campaigns, then, is to get their supporters to take a day off; come to Ames, Iowa, which is just north of the state capitol, Des Monies; and listen to speeches from the field of Republican presidential contenders. After that, the attendees at the straw poll, who have each paid $25 a head to participate, cast ballots for whomever they favor for the Republican presidential nomination. In 1999 as in the past, the outcome had no bearing on the results of the caucus, which were still months away, on January 24, 2000.

Nevertheless, the exercise was seen as an early indicator of which candidates were able to build grassroots organizations in the state and motivate their supporters to travel to Ames, just as they would have to be motivated to go out in the dead of a winter night on January 24 to attend their neighborhood caucus. Note that more than four hundred reporters usually cover this event as well.

These factors forced all the Republicans presidential candidates, except McCain who had already announced that he was not going to contest the Iowa caucuses, to shift into high gear for the straw poll. But that took money, something only two candidates, Bush and magazine publisher Steve Forbes, possessed at that point. It is widely believed that

Forbes spent some $700,000 on this exercise alone—which just a few years ago would have been a presidential candidate's entire budget for the actual Iowa caucuses.

How can one spend so much money on an event that has only symbolic importance? For starters, the campaigns usually pay for their supporters' $25 tickets. Then there is the cost of hours and hours of phone banks, run by the campaigns to find people who are willing to give up a summer Saturday to travel to the straw poll. Then there are the buses chartered by the campaigns to bring their supporters to Ames. And then there are the hospitality tents that the campaigns run to care and feed their supporters before the speeches and the actual poll.

Forbes's tent was so elaborate that one Bush supporter called it "Chateau Forbes." But do not think that the Bush campaign was doing this event on the cheap. His campaign had paid the Iowa State party $40,000 to rent the most desirable *space* for this campaign tent, right outside the auditorium where the candidates would deliver their speeches. And the Bush people were serving barbecue meals to anyone who wandered by, just like Forbes. One Bush operative told me that "we served more meals than we got votes." But Bush did win the straw poll, while Forbes finished second, followed by Elizabeth Dole in third.

Technically, this was a meaningless event. The caucuses were still about five months away. Nevertheless, it had very real impact. A few days after finishing a disappointing sixth place, Lamar Alexander, the former governor of Tennessee, withdrew from the race. Alexander was a competent politician who had run for the 1996 Republican presidential nomination and finished a close third in the all-important New Hampshire primary. He had established some credibility in that race and was seen as a serious contender in 2000. But he could never raise the requisite funds. Remember, the crush of primaries that were going to be held on March 7 required the candidates to build a large war chest in 1999, so they would not be caught short subsequently. At least, that was the prevailing wisdom at the time.

A few days before the straw poll, Alexander was on a conference call with the leadership of his campaign. His finance chairman, Ted Welch, told him flatly that anything less than a third-place finish, near the top of the pack, would be disastrous. Welch, who had had to struggle to raise a handful of $1,000 checks to keep Alexander's campaign afloat in the summer, knew that without the perception of victory or at least of a solid showing, even Alexander's diehard supporters would shut their wallets. So, after he finished sixth, Alexander withdrew from the race.

There is an old saying in nominating contest politics, that you never lose, you simply run out of money. What was different about the 2000 race is that this kind of winnowing was taking place before any real votes were cast. Indeed, substantial Republican candidates would soon follow Alexander's course and leave the Republican race unusually early.

Not much later, Dan Quayle, former vice president, with an eighth place showing in Iowa, followed suit. Even Mrs. Dole, who had finished third in the straw poll and won a burst of media coverage for what was taken to be an unexpectedly strong showing, bowed out. Both Quayle and Dole cited the inability to raise sufficient funds to keep up with Bush and Forbes as the main reason they were withdrawing.

All told, six candidates got out of the Republican presidential race before the end of 1999. Alexander, Dole, and Quayle were joined by John Kasich, a congressman from Ohio, Bob Smith, a senator from New Hampshire, and Pat Buchanan, the conservative political commentator who opted to run for the Reform Party nomination. This kind of attrition, the year before the caucuses and primaries, was unprecedented in presidential nominating politics. It strikes me as powerful evidence that the "invisible primary" phase of the campaign has taken on even more importance in presidential politics. In effect, the winnowing process, which normally occurs after the Iowa caucuses with candidates who fare poorly, was now taking place *before* Iowa.

This is not to say that actual campaigning in presidential 2000 did not matter. How candidates react in the heat of battle, how they handle debates, the tactical and strategic decisions they and their advisers make to adapt to changing circumstances and new issues—all are vitally important factors to their eventual success of failure. (If it did not matter, I would probably be out of a job, as my magazine's readers remain quite interested in such things.) The case to make for 2000, though, is that the political dynamics of the invisible primary set the table, so to speak, for the Republican contest. Bush emerged as the favorite of the party establishment, and McCain became the insurgent, all before a single delegate had been selected.

The story of the rise of Vice President Gore in the invisible primary on the Democratic side, 2000, is actually a story of rise, fall, and rise. At the start, the impression of nearly all of Gore's potential rivals that he would be unbeatable was obviously a great benefit to him. Every time a Democrat like Gephardt and Kerrey and others said they that they would *not* enter the race, the perception built that the vice president's nomination was inevitable. Yet there is still a difference between working to project the sense of inevitability and acting and campaigning as if you are indeed inevitable. Gore adopted the latter stance in 1999, and it ended up costing him many sleepless nights in the invisible primary.

As winter turned to spring, the trial heats pairing Bush and Gore began to bear out the findings of the exit polls on election night 1998. Bush was beating Gore handily. Initially, Gore's campaign dismissed the results of these trial heats. "It's too early for these polls to mean anything," his campaign managers said. Sometimes, they asserted that there were technical problems in the questionnaires or the surveys. But these kinds of responses began to come across to party insiders as arrogance.

That seemed to fit a larger picture of the Gore campaign, as a kind of out-of-touch, corporate enterprise. He had a $60,000-a-month office on K Street in Washington, D.C. And this seemed appropriate, too, because many of Gore's key campaign advisers and strategists were either lobbyists or members of some other part of the influence industry that has many of its offices on K Street.

Still, Gore remained far ahead of Bill Bradley in polls of Democrats on who they supported for the Democratic nomination. So the vice president and some of his advisers remained reluctant to attack Bradley. Why give him any free attention? Better to stay above the fray. Indeed, even into the early summer, Gore personally felt that Bradley might withdraw from the race, as he encountered the difficulty of raising money in the face of nearly the entire party establishment, which was backing the vice president.

Meanwhile, the vice president's campaign took on the trappings of an imperial candidacy. On the one hand, there is nothing quite so impressive as to arrive in Air Force Two and then have police escorts to and from campaign stops. White House advance people and the secret service move you smoothly through crowds from podium to limousine, and that nearly always guarantees coverage on the local news. But the whole retinue can sometimes get in the way of the personal campaigning that is so important in early states like Iowa and New Hampshire, where voters expect candidates to lavish attention on them.

Sensing that his campaign was growing listless, Gore stunned nearly all of Washington and everyone on his staff in May when he appointed Tony Coelho, a former Democratic leader in the House of Representatives from the 1980s, to become chairman of his campaign. The vice president knew Coelho from the time they had spent together in the House and during 1994, when Coelho was an unofficial adviser to President Clinton. But Coelho's ascent, while it did impose some order and a hierarchy in the campaign that had not existed before, did not turn around the vice president's fortunes. At least, he continued to lag badly behind Bush in the general election trial heat polls. And the campaign still felt "top heavy," at one point calling on the services of six pollsters.

Even worse, Bill Bradley was now gaining on him. One of the remarkable aspects of the Bradley campaign was the way that the former Rhodes scholar, professional basketball player, and senator was able to raise as much money as Al Gore. When Gore and Bradley filed their campaign finance reports in July for the first half of the year, Gore had raised more, it is true, but he had also spent more on his campaign apparatus. Bradley was only a few million short of Gore in terms of cash on hand or in the bank. It became clear to Gore and his aides that Bradley was not going to be eased of the race by any sense of the vice president's inevitability.

Then, on September 5, the vice president woke up to a poll in the *Boston Globe* that showed that Bradley was running even with him in New Hampshire. If Bradley could capture the first-in-the-nation primary, it would topple the proud tower of the Gore campaign and cause Democrats to abandon his candidacy. Gore himself had sensed that he needed to shake things up further. So he had his entire campaign apparatus abandon the seraglios of Washington, where backbiting among the vice president's advisers was rampant and quickly reported in the press, and moved a much-streamlined organization to Nashville, in his home state of Tennessee.

To give you a sense of what the mood was like around Washington at the time, one Democratic consultant joked to me, on the day that Gore announced his new headquarters would be in Nashville: "Well, that's just one less move he'll have to make after the election." Gore and Coelho also shook up the campaign staff and brought on a new team of consultants schooled in the art of playing offense. In a focus group setting, they tested lines of attack that Gore now had to use against his surging challenger, Bill Bradley.

Attacking remained something of a dilemma for the vice president: he was good at it, but sometimes he came across as too political and insincere when he was on the offensive. But what the Gore campaign's focus groups found was that when Gore criticized the Bradley health care plan as wrecking Medicaid, the health service for the poor in the United States, and endangering Medicare, the health service for the elderly, these rank-and-file Democratic voters responded favorably. They saw this critique not so much as attacking Bradley, but rather as fighting for them and their programs.

In the fall, the Gore campaign was resurrected. The new slogan of his campaign, tested in those focus groups, became "Stand and fight," which was also a reference to the fact that Bradley did not stand for reelection to the Senate in 1996, knowing that the Republicans were in the majority after the 1994 midterm elections. About this time, Gore also won the support of the AFL–CIO, the parent body of the industrial, service sector, and public employee unions. This was an endorsement that Gore had worked hard for, having wooed dozens of labor leaders and spoken at countless union halls and state conventions throughout 1999, and even earlier. The National Education Association, the largest teachers union in the United States, followed suit. Support from the unions would provide critical political foot soldiers for Gore's campaign apparatus.

In their first debate in October, Gore, who had largely been ignoring Bradley for much of the year, directly assailed his health care plan as a risky enterprise that would not only endanger Medicaid and Medicare, but would also break the budget because of its costs. When it came time for Bradley to reply, he blithely said, "Well Al, you have your numbers, and I have mine." That was it. No more response. It seemed as though it was beneath Bradley to respond to Gore's attacks. Indeed, more than one observer said that Bradley seemed to be approaching the campaign as though he were an Oxford don.

So Gore kept attacking. When Bradley finally ended up replying in kind, digging back into Gore's record in Congress in the 1970s and 1980s and correctly pointing out that the vice president had opposed some gun control and abortion rights legislation, Bradley came across as petty and Gore was able to play the role of wounded victim. But Gore, from his side, never took anything lying down. For instance, when Bradley tried to attack him for not having a sterling record on abortion rights, the vice president was able to call on others to vouch for him.

Here was a tangible benefit of having lined up all those endorsements from his fellow Democrats in 1999. The day after Bradley began unloading his charges, prominent Democratic women members of Congress who were well identified with the abortion rights issue came to Gore's defense. They held news conferences. They did interviews. A few even traveled to New Hampshire to campaign for the vice president.

Had Bradley been able to establish himself as the antiestablishment candidate, he might have been able to gain some political advantage by mocking the Gore defenders as being just all the king's men. But Bradley had made a fatal mistake at the end of the invisible primary. In December 1999, he joined John McCain on the same podium in New

Hampshire, where both men swore their fidelity to campaign finance reform.

At the time, it did not seem like such a bad move. Bradley shared with McCain considerable media attention from this unusual bipartisan presidential campaign event. But it also sent a signal to independents in New Hampshire, who tend to vote more heavily in the Democratic primary, that maybe McCain was okay. After all, if a respected liberal like Bradley would share the stage with McCain, maybe he was not that conservative.

Bradley's campaign never thereafter kicked into high gear, and McCain's did. Oftentimes, independents, who do not have particular ties to either party, will back a candidate whose campaign is generating the most excitement and who looks like he may win. After all, everybody wants his or her vote to count. On primary day in New Hampshire, a lot of independents, who can vote in either the Republican or the Democratic presidential primary, opted to back McCain, whose campaign against Bush was surging. And that is how McCain won the New Hampshire primary and, for a moment, became a real threat to George W. Bush.

THE HIDDEN CAMPAIGN 2000

Having failed to establish his candidacy in New Hampshire, a state where he once had been expected to beat Al Gore, the Bradley campaign became a deathwatch. Five weeks later, Gore would defeat him in all fifteen states that held a Democratic primary on March 7. Two days later, Bradley withdrew from the race. As it turned out, there was only room for one insurgent in the entire presidential race, Democratic and Republican.

John McCain did go on to give Bush some anxious moments in the Republican race. Indeed, he actually defeated the Texan in seven Republican primaries. But in the end, Bush's advantages in money and support from elected Republican officials around the country, which he had nurtured in the invisible primary, proved to be decisive. The result was two major-party presidential nominees and one future president. But the result was also what I call the "hidden campaign" of the presidential contest, a phase that follows the primaries and continues through the two national party conventions.

Normally, this is the apparent "lull" between the two main rounds of the presidential race, the primary contests and the general election campaign, traditionally beginning on Labor Day, at the start of September. On the surface, this is usually just a period of preliminary jousting between the two de facto nominees. That is because, more often than not, at least one of those two candidates is still mopping up the last resistance of primary opponents. Simultaneously, both of the standard-bearers are looking for a break from the rigorous pace they have kept during the primary season.

And once the decisive battles of the primaries are over, most voters want a break from politics too. Some will tune back into the race during the two national conventions in late summer. Most will wait until the fall. The year 2000 was nevertheless a bit different, and the hidden campaign bulked consequently larger. Neither Bush nor Gore had to spend time mopping up opposition within their own party; both had vanquished their primary rivals by March 8. Neither of the two nominating contests had been marked by deep ideological splits; neither Bush nor Gore needed to spend time making peace with a disaffected wing inside their own party. They had both won their nominations because they had been so effective in the invisible primary, securing the broad support of their respective party's establishment.

Yet both candidates had work to do. As a result, the hidden campaign of 2000 would not actually be conducted behind the curtains. Most citizens, and indeed most journalists, might look away. But the events of that campaign remained available to those who wanted to see.

Although Bush had begun the contest with a comfortable lead over Gore in trial heat polls for the general election, by the end of the primaries that lead had all but vanished. In a few surveys, Gore was actually ahead. To defeat McCain, Bush had had to rally the conservative base in the Republican Party. Not only was McCain bitter over what he viewed as the hard-edged tactics employed by Bush to defeat him, but Bush was now seen as having swung too far to the right to be able to win in the fall. "Amid this Republican wreckage, Gore is now golden," wrote a *New York Daily News* columnist. "Bush has more baggage than Gore as they start White House Marathon" was the headline in the *Boston Globe*.

Even reporters from the other side of the Atlantic got into the act. "The real problem for Mr. Bush is that he seems lightweight," said Andrew Marshall in *The Independent*. "Mr. Gore has emerged from the early primary elections in far better shape than Mr. Bush," wrote David Wastell for the *Sunday Telegraph*. "Bush will win the Republican nomination, but at a hefty price; Gore has all but won the Democratic nomination, and in the process the Vice President has transformed himself into a far more potent candidate," ventured Ben MacIntyre in *The Times.*

To deal with these perception problems, Bush took to the policy road. He literally overwhelmed us with new initiatives, big and small. And in a very energetic way, he addressed issues that Republican presidential candidates normally shy away from, like education and health care. Simply by tackling issues that are normally the province of Democrats, with what seemed like a new pronouncement every week, Bush was able to position himself back in the center.

"We did more of them than probably originally planned," said Bush's top media adviser Mark McKinnon. "We really came to understand how you can drive news with policy. The press is hungry for a story every day of the presidential campaign. Strategically, you want it on policy, not process, because if it's on process [the internal decision making of a campaign], it's usually bad," said McKinnon. "Policy stories," he said, "give the sharks something to digest and chew on."

This was not, however, just a political gambit. George W. Bush was using the time to develop his governing agenda. For instance, he laid out his rationale for a robust National Missile Defense (NMD) in a major foreign policy address in May. At that event in Washington, he was flanked by a handful of national security advisers, including Donald Rumsfeld. Later, as the U.S. Secretary of Defense, Rumsfeld would receive the task of telling European defense officials that the United States had a "moral duty" to deploy NMD, that Bush had been serious.

In May, Bush also offered a general but very venturesome outline for reforming Social Security, the old-age insurance fund that is the most popular entitlement program in the United States. Bush proposed allowing individuals to divert a portion of their Social Security payments into personal accounts, to be invested in the stock market. The old adage was that Social Security was the "third rail" of American politics—when politicians touched it, they died. But Bush did not. Instead, while they quibbled with the lack of details, editorial pages and nonpartisan experts generally greeted his proposal as a serious response to demographic trends in the United States that show that without some sort of reform, the system will eventually collapse.

One other strong piece of evidence that Bush's Social Security proposal was effective was the response from his opponent. Prior to the point when Bush outlined his plan, Gore had already asserted that the system did not need to be overhauled and that it should not in any case be privatized in any way. After Bush released his outline, Gore hit hard, saying that families' retirement money would be lost in "stock market roulette." Then, after about three weeks of attacks, Gore unveiled his own plan, "Social Security plus." Individuals could contribute to a voluntary savings account; receive a matching contribution from the government, paid for out of general revenue funds not Social Security payments; and then take this pool of money and invest it in a broad-based stock or bond fund.

Al Gore also needed to use this phase of the campaign to flesh out his vision for the country. In effect, he had won the Democratic nomination on the strength of his support from the party establishment and the effectiveness of his attacks on Bill Bradley. "There was a huge problem with message," said his campaign manager, Tad Devine. "It hadn't been refined in a way that was powerful enough to win more votes in a general election." Complicating Gore's task was the need to identify himself with the successes of the Clinton Administration, particularly the strength of the economy, without being identified with the president himself. Clinton had a high job-approval rating, but his scandals were a substantial negative with many voters.

Gore finally seemed to get on track in June. He shook up his campaign staff again when his chairman, Tony Coelho, resigned citing poor health. At the same time, the Gore campaign launched its "Peace and prosperity" theme package. Gore pointed to the success of the economy, but he also offered new prescriptions for protecting the environment and shoring up Medicare, the health insurance program for the elderly. And, as mentioned earlier, he came up with a new plan for Social Security. "If he had succeeded in the election, that would have been the time that his agenda for the nation was developed," said Devine.

Perhaps most importantly, he found his own voice. The populist rhetoric that Gore used in his very effective acceptance speech at the Democratic National Convention in August was debuted during this phase of the campaign. It was at rallies during this time that he first used his people-not-the-powerful line, to highlight his support for average Americans as opposed to big drug companies and health management organizations, the private medical services that have been criticized for restricting health care for their patients. In a sense, both Bush and Gore were fleshing out and completing their manifestos for governing in the policy speeches that they both made in the spring and early summer.

In theory, the Republican and Democratic activists who are delegates to their respective national party conventions draw up the official party platforms. To be sure, the two presidential nominees of 2000, George Bush and Al Gore, had considerable influence over the practical drafting of these documents. But sometimes, convention delegates who represent powerful constituent groups in the party—abortion rights opponents in the Republican Party or labor union officials in the Democratic Party—will be able to tailor a plank to reflect their respective group's position, and not that of the presidential nominee.

If this modification is hugely at odds with where the presidential candidate stands, his operatives will attempt to use their influence with the rest of the delegates to strike it down. But if it is not a major challenge to the nominee, he will simply ignore it. When Bob Dole, the Republican presidential nominee of 1996, was asked about the more restrictive abortion language in that year's party platform, Dole confessed to reporters he had not read it—and left everyone with the impression that he never would.

Delegates to the Republican convention are more conservative than regular Republican voters, just as delegates to the Democratic convention are more liberal than rank-and-file Democrats. Technically, you could say that at the two summer conventions, the candidates who have prevailed in the primaries come before these delegates, who formally nominate them to be their standard-bearers in the general election campaign that occurs in the fall. But the modern convention really has little to do with addressing party activists.

Even though the major television networks have dramatically cut back the airtime they devote to these quadrennial party gatherings, the two nominees use the convention stage instead to address and appeal to regular voters, particularly the so-called swing voters—that is, the soccer moms of America or the "Worchester women" of Britain. Indeed, the relationship between the convention and the general election is now seen as a seamless one by the nominees and their chief strategists. "The convention used to be a separate stop along the way for a candidate," said Bush's convention manger, Andy Card, who is now White House chief of staff. As Devine, Gore's campaign manager, put it this way: "We never viewed the convention as four days, but four weeks. . . . We kept it going through Labor Day."

The chief goal of the Bush campaign at the Republican convention in Philadelphia was to change the image of the party. And the way to do that was to make the convention about Bush, not the party. For six years, following the Republican takeover of the House of Representatives and the Senate in the 1994 midterm elections, the party's hard-edged conservative congressional leadership, most particularly in the form of House Speaker Newt Gingrich, had succeeded in defining the party in policy terms for the general public. In this, they had been remarkably successful.

The job of the Bush team at their convention, as they saw it, was to escape this definition. "We knew it would be easier to define George Bush than redefine the Republican Party," said Bush's chief media strategist McKinnon. "We wanted to take the party to him, not him to the party."

Initially, it was the goal of the Bush campaign to have not a single elected Republican official address the convention, other than Bush. They eventually relented enough to allow McCain to have a major speaking slot. Otherwise, the tone in Philadelphia was set on the first night of the convention. It was the first time that the wife of a first-time presidential nominee addressed the delegates (and the nation) in prime time. While Laura Bush did talk about education—she was a former school librarian—the real focus of her remarks was not public policy. Her primary mission was to talk about the character of her husband. For average voters, she could have more credibility on this topic than any politician.

The next person who spoke that night was General Colin Powell, the former Chairman of the Joint Chiefs of Staff, whose popularity with Americans was unmatched by any elected official. Powell had also spoken on the opening night of the 1996 Republican convention, the one that nominated Bob Dole. In that speech four years earlier, Powell mentioned the words "Republican" or "Republican Party" sixteen times; in his 2000 speech, he referenced the party only twice. Conversely, in 1996, he mentioned nominee Dole's name only three times in his opening remarks; he referred to Bush more than a dozen times in Philadelphia.

The Bush campaign did not write General Powell's speech for him that night, but it was not just coincidence that his remarks followed the overall script for the convention either. Bush's advisers told all the featured speakers that whenever possible, they should weave personal observations about Bush into their comments. In an otherwise provocative and iconoclastic speech, Powell obviously found this advice easy to take.

Al Gore also had work to do at his convention. Like all vice presidents, he had to establish that he was really his own man. That meant, first, the "Clinton issue." This was handled in a carefully choreographed manner. Bill Clinton addressed the Democratic convention in Los Angeles on its opening night. He pointed to the success of the economy; praised Gore, albeit briefly; and then literally left town. The next day, Clinton flew to Michigan, where he met Gore and symbolically handed over the reigns of the party. Only after that did Gore fly to Los Angeles.

Still, Gore's many previous reinventions of himself had made the public skeptical about what he really believed. So, the story had to be completed on the last night of the Democratic convention, when he gave his acceptance speech. Early in his remarks, the vice president said "I am my own man," and went on to give a rousing address, saying quite directly that he would not rest on the laurels of the good economy. Even his very public embrace with his wife, Tipper, as he stepped up to the convention podium, seemed finally to give Gore the authenticity he had not been able to establish with the electorate. "The voters had been reading all these who-is-he stories in the press," said his convention manager, Marcia Hale. "And he gave a speech that made clear who he was."

As late as 1968, the outcomes of presidential nominating contests were still being decided—or at least ultimately confirmed—at national party conventions. After that, the growth of presidential primaries made the backroom deal-makers largely irrelevant to the nominating process. It is a story that Byron Shafer has told well. Suffice it to say that the conventions themselves became little more than free television time for the political parties, to showcase the nominee. The deliberative role of conventions was much reduced, by voters in the primaries who now held the power to send delegates to these quadrennial gatherings.

Many political professionals in the United States, as well as some academics, have bemoaned the demise of the deliberative party convention. Among other features, it provided an opportunity for party leaders to exercise a kind of peer review and select a nominee whose strengths and weaknesses they knew from personal experience. Well, those people should be happy with the results of the invisible primary in 2000. In an unprecedented manner, Republican and Democratic elected officials, constituency group leaders, and fund-raisers coalesced around the two nominees. And this support was critical to both George W. Bush and Al Gore in order to prevail in the quest for their respective party's presidential nomination.

In a way, the invisible primary in the 2000 campaign resurrected the smoke-filled rooms of convention days gone past. The only difference being that the conversations of these party elites were conducted in Austin or Nashville, at private meetings in primary states around the country, or maybe just on conference calls.

It is a little harder to come up with such a definitive finding about the impact of the postprimary, pregeneral-election phase of the 2000 presidential contest, what I call the hidden campaign. Setting aside the decision by the U.S. Supreme Court last December, senior operatives in both the Bush and Gore campaigns believe that the decisive event of the general election was the first presidential debate. The vice president's staggeringly poor performance—his condescending manner and minor dissembling—reconnected voters to the Al Gore they did not like. For many voters, the aura of authenticity that Gore had gained with his convention speech disappeared, while old doubts about his political character were revived.

Instead of being on the defensive in the next two debates, Bush could win by letting his appealing personality come through and by simply holding his own in the give-and-take with Gore. "People wanted to like Bush," said Bush media adviser McKinnon. "In the debates, people said, 'Okay, he can do this.'" But Gore's stumble in the debates, which probably should have killed him, did not. A combined analysis off all the public polls after the convention, conducted by Bush's pollster, shows that during the debates, Bush's aggregate advantage never rose above 4.2 percent. Indeed, within a few days after that third debate, his edge over Gore again declined.

Likewise, before the debates, when Gore was still surging in the wake of his convention and Bush was stumbling in the period his aides referred to as "Black September," the combined analysis showed that Bush never trailed Gore by more than 3.4 percent. I think this means that during the hidden campaign, both candidates established a floor of support, a foundation for the fall campaign that was solid enough to withstand the downdrafts and setbacks that would have doomed less mature candidacies.

Think about it this way: When there is bad news in the high-tech world, IBM's stock price may fall 5 percent, and that is a lot of money. Yet at the same time, the value of the less established dot.com will collapse, and it may never recover. What happened in 2000 is that after that hidden campaign, both Bush and Gore were in a strong enough position to win the White House. Indeed, given the tortuous outcome of the election last year, it may be hard to argue that either one of those candidates really lost.

4

Dynamics of the 2000 Campaign:
Preliminary Soundings

Richard Johnston, University of British Columbia
Michael G. Hagen, University of Pennsylvania
Kathleen Hall Jamieson, University of Pennsylvania

The 2000 election was one of the closest in history, and the campaign was one of the few since the dawn of polling to see the lead change hands more than once after Labor Day.[1] Even if we concede that most presidential elections are highly predictable, if only because most are one-sided, *this*, surely, was a campaign that mattered. It was also a campaign that was closely scrutinized. From mid-September on, it was possible in principle for an attentive citizen to get a daily update on the horse race.[2]

Also in the field every day was the first-ever academic "tracking poll," the Annenberg Year 2000 Rolling Cross-Section Survey. This survey combined continuous fieldwork with an elaborate interview instrument, a combination that yields an enormous advantage over both commercial polls and academic surveys. This chapter gives only a foretaste of its power. The chapter starts with a brief account of the study, and then describes the course of vote intentions from July to November. The narrative of vote intention is highly suggestive by itself of the causes of dynamics. We supplement the narrative with a nod toward two factors that were almost certainly critical but that did not appear on the surface of events: first, voters' perceptions of candidates, and second, the evolution of a specific issue. We conclude with thoughts about the speed with which campaign events unfold.

THE ANNENBERG STUDY

The Annenberg 2000 Election Study comprised one hundred thousand interviews with over eighty thousand voting-age respondents, with fieldwork under the management of Princeton Survey Research Associates (PSRA)[3] and Schulman Ronca Bucuvalas, Inc. (SRBI).[4] Its largest single element is the National Continuous Monitor, which was in the field in almost unbroken fashion from November 1999 to January 2001. Apart from sheer scale, the distinctive feature of the Monitor was its manner of release to the field. All telephone numbers were generated at random and then assigned to "replicates," also at random. Each replicate thus was a representative subsample of the larger, total sample, with enough randomly generated telephone numbers to yield fifty completed interviews over a two-week clearance period.

Replicates were then released to field day by day, at least one per day and often more. By clearing each replicate the same way (allowing for seasonal variation in accessibility), the day on which a respondent happened to be interviewed became as much a product of random forces as that person's initial selection for the overall sample was. The density of interviewing could also vary from period to period without loss of this random character.[5] This chapter draws on the period of highest density, July to election day, when six replicates, enough to yield three hundred completed interviews, were released to the field each day.

THE HORSE RACE

Figure 4.1 portrays the course of vote intentions for the major candidates from late July to election day.[6] The rough plot represents daily values, to which we refer frequently. Because sampling error creates surplus vertical flux in the daily plot, we also superimpose a smoothed tracking, in this case by "loess" with a bandwidth of 15 percent.

Evidently, Al Gore was behind by late July and fell even further behind with the Republican National Convention.[7] The Democratic National Convention neutralized the impact of the Republican one and then delivered Gore a lead, which he essentially held until late September. By October, Gore had fallen behind, and only at the end did he

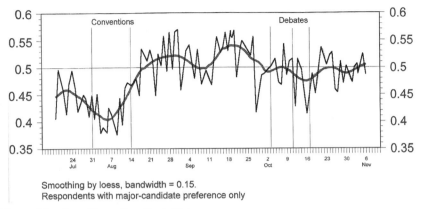

Smoothing by loess, bandwidth = 0.15.
Respondents with major-candidate preference only

Figure 4.1   Gore Share, Two-Party Vote

recover. This much is probably familiar as narrative, and it need not occasion much theoretically motivated hand-wringing. But closer examination sheds new light on the operation of familiar events and directs attention to unanticipated places. First, consider the impact of the most highly visible events.

Exactly as we should expect, the Democratic convention had a greater impact than the Republican one. Where the Republican event boosted George W. Bush's share by five or six points, the Democratic convention gave Al Gore a boost of ten to twelve points. This difference corresponds to a pattern identified by Thomas M. Holbrook: the worse a party's share of vote intentions relative to the share predicted for it by forecasting models applied to that year, the bigger that party's convention "bounce."[8] All predictions, even the revisionist "postdiction" by Larry M. Bartels and John Zaller,[9] were for a Democratic win. The implication, then, is that in July the system was already leaning "too far" to the Republican side, such that the possible impact of that party's convention was severely constrained. The Democratic event was not so constrained.

If this much should be unsurprising to historically minded observers, the same cannot be said for the exact time-path for each convention's effect. The Annenberg survey's high resolution reveals that the convention effect has two parts, and that the second part enjoys a remarkably rapid onset. These points come out of inspection of the daily data, without benefit of smoothing. The first impact predates the convention itself, and seems to be an effect of the vice presidential nomination. Four days before the Republicans convened, the Gore share dropped to the low 40s. Before that, it had exhibited considerable volatility, but readings in the high 40s were as ubiquitous as those lower in the range. From July 26, however, the share's oscillations were confined to the 40 to 45 percent range, and stayed there until August 2.

Roughly the same sequence occurred in the run-up to the Democratic convention. On either August 10 or 12, the Gore share surged, instantly undoing all damage from the Republican event. The new level was sustained until August 17. It seems natural to attribute the dramatic Democratic surge to the inspired choice of Joe Lieberman. The larger narrative suggests a simpler and more generalizable interpretation: the choice of a vice presidential nominee, almost regardless of party or person, generates positive coverage, which in turn induces a surge in support for the ticket.[10] The timing of the Democratic event reproduces almost exactly that for the Republican event. That the amplitude was greater reflects the fact that the system was more out of equilibrium, so to speak, after the Republican convention than before.

Of course, vice presidential nominations do not exhaust the convention narrative. For each party, there also occurred a surge specific to the convention itself. In each case, the surge coincided with the nominee's acceptance speech and had all its effect immediately. On the fourth day of the Republican convention, the Gore share dropped from the low-to-mid 40s to below 40 percent. No further decay appeared. On the Democratic side, the overnight surge came the day following Gore's acceptance speech. As with the earlier pulse, the impact was almost immediate.

Detecting debate effects takes more work and generally yields weaker returns. But impact can be found. It is delayed, suggesting that effects are mediated. What matters is not so much the debate itself as what is made of the debate in subsequent media commentary. A debate effect, where it occurs, is commonly ephemeral. Is this because the impulse is inherently transitory, fated to decay on its own? Or does it reflect the fact that debates are closely spaced, such that earlier debate effects are actively erased by later ones? This opens up the possibility that the last debate is qualitatively different.

The first debate was commonly interpreted as a Bush victory, but if it moved the horse race, it did so only after a three-day lag and only for a couple of days. Any impact it might have had was gone *before* the second debate, suggesting weak induction all along. The second presidential debate, in contrast, *did* have an adverse impact on Gore, and this impact endured to the next debate. Again, the onset seems delayed, but there is no mistaking the direction in the daily tracking. The smoothed line also picks up Gore's dip. The third debate clearly helped Gore. Again, the onset was delayed, but when the surge came it probably gave him the lead back, at least for a while. Although the lead subsequently changed hands, Gore's competitive position had clearly improved.

Why did Gore's September lead collapse? We can start with when it collapsed. In journalistic commentary, much was made of the first debate. It does seem true that that event had an adverse impact on the Gore share. But our tracking suggests that the biggest impact had already occurred, indeed that Gore was already making a partial recovery from that earlier impact. The big drop occurred between September 26 and 27. The overnight impact was truly massive, ten to fifteen points, well outside the 95 percent confidence interval for a daily sample. The negative impulse began to decay immediately, but was never completely dissipated. By the eve of the first debate, Gore was still about five points behind his position of late September. Whatever importance we attach to the debates, especially the last one, none comes close to having an effect as strategically important as this late-September shift.

Other shifts, although not as critical as the September 26–27 one, also merit scrutiny. One sequence came in early September. Although Gore was basically ahead from his acceptance speech to September 26, the ride was not entirely smooth. By our reckoning he fell behind—at least fell into a tie—right after Labor Day. His recovery occurred between September 11 and 12 and took him to still greater heights. Both the decline and the recovery were swift. The second sequence is the recovery after the last debate. Although there seems no question that Gore's fortunes generally improved in this period, their progress was uneven. Gore fell back between October 24 and 25 and only reached the 50 percent threshold on the campaign's very last weekend.

THE CAMPAIGN AND THE CANDIDATES

Gore had a big lead, blew the lead, and then drew back even. If this is the underlying dynamic of the campaign, part of the explanation for it lies in voters' judgments on the candidates as persons. Gore lost his lead because voters came to doubt his character. Then, the modest advantage bequeathed to Bush by Gore's character problem was itself erased as voters came to doubt Bush's competence. This section outlines a circumstantial case.

The case rests on a tracking of respondents' perceptions of key candidate attributes. In the Annenberg study, these are captured by trait ratings directly modeled on a battery in the National Election Study.[11] Respondents rated candidates on five traits, where each trait was represented by an adjective or an adjectival phrase, in the July–November period. Here we focus on two: "honest," an indication of character, and "knowledgeable," an indication of competence.

These two traits differentiated the candidates sharply, and were themselves the most sharply differentiated of all traits within each candidate's profile. Response to these items, thus, was neither mere partisanship nor liking-disliking by another name. By election day, Gore enjoyed a huge advantage over Bush in perceptions of competence, but Bush commanded an equally huge advantage in perceptions of character. On the day, as figure 4.2 shows, voters preoccupied with the candidates as individuals faced a huge trade-off.

How voters got to this trade-off is also revealed by figure 4.2, and this takes us back to campaign dynamics. Early shifts in candidate perception, from July to roughly mid-September, indicate mainly a general repositioning around the conventions. For each candidate, each trait moves roughly synchronically with the other trait. Bush gets better on both traits around the Republican convention and then embarks on a gradual slide helped along by the Democratic convention.

At the peak, Bush seemed a tiny bit more knowledgeable than honest,[12] but this reflects the fact that respondents resist the possibility that a candidate for major public office is *not* knowledgeable. At this peak, he almost rivaled Gore for perceived competence. Gore never seemed more honest than knowledgeable, but otherwise July–September shifts in his character and competence ratings were of similar timing and direction, if not magnitude. Both ratings surged after the Democratic convention, spectacularly so for "honesty," such that Bush's character advantage was erased even as Gore's competence advantage expanded.

In late September, perceptions of Gore changed dramatically. Respondents never ceased to see him as knowledgeable. But his reputation for honesty collapsed. Smoothed tracking has the drop beginning on September 16 and continuing seemingly without break until about October 10. Underlying daily data indicate that the real start of the drop was probably September 20. They also make clear that the drop was accelerated by the first debate. After October 10 or so, perceptions of Gore dropped no further. This must have been small comfort, for now the typical respondent saw Gore in a worse light than before the Republican convention. On this dimension, of course, Gore was far behind Bush.

The narrative of the campaign reveals no single event in the days

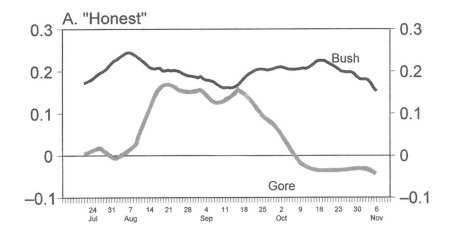

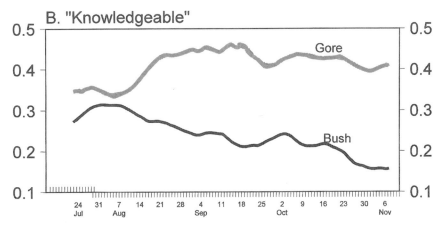

Loess smoothing, bandwidth = 0.15.
Respondents with a major-candidate preference only

Figure 4.2   The Critical Traits

before the collapse of Gore's character perception. The first debate did produce character comment, mainly generated by Gore's statements about crowding in Florida classrooms and the exact identity of his traveling companions to Texas disasters. But the debate only accelerated the already precipitous drop. What we do know about the days around September 20 is that Gore was dogged by, first, the resurrection of a story he had told about his mother's dog's medicine and, second, by controversy over his demand for the release of oil from the Strategic

Petroleum Reserve. If these news events are the key to voter reevaluations of Gore, substantiating and understanding their impact will take some doing. It suffices for the moment to note how powerful the impact evidently can be from so ephemeral a force.

And this impact seems critical to the whole campaign. It is hard to believe that had Gore not suffered such a perceptual reverse, he would have lost the election. If the basic story is that Gore was ahead in September and behind in October, the one big background factor that reproduces essentially this structure is his reputation for honesty. Putting things this way implies that the thing to explain is why Gore dropped from September to October. Perhaps the question is how he was able to jack his character perceptions up so much between July and August. Either way, the pattern is a challenge to both theory and empirical practice.

By the time Gore's character ratings began to plummet, Bush's competence ratings had been sliding steadily for over a month. Whatever modest boost the Republican convention gave him had more than dissipated. Then, for the next month, no further damage was done. Right after the last debate, however, a marked decline set in, such that about one-third of the total postconvention decay occurred in the last two weeks of October. The daily data underlying figure 4.2 make clear that the debate itself is the point of discontinuity.

Bush's postdebate slump may be more general than for perceptions of his competence. The top panel of figure 4.2 indicates that his honesty ratings also slumped, and by about as much. Given that Bush's honesty rating had hardly moved before the last debate, this event accounts for essentially Bush's entire campaign-period shift. And these late declines for Bush may explain some of the roughly contemporaneous Republican decline and Democratic recovery.

SOCIAL SECURITY AND THE STOCK MARKET

Many issues were debated in the campaign, and the issue basis of the choice is a critical question. Few issues exhibited *dynamic* variation, however. Typically, voters knew their own positions and did not change them. Similarly, voters could impute a position on each issue to each candidate, and imputations also tended not to shift. Most respondents most of the time made the "correct" imputation. When they failed, it was either because they projected their own opinion onto the already-favored candidate or the opposite position onto a disfavored one, or because they simply imposed a partisan stereotype.

The 2000 campaign featured a major exception, however, and this exception wonderfully exemplifies learning in a campaign. Voters had to learn where the candidate stood, Al Gore especially. Learning where the candidates stood then helped voters determine where they themselves should stand. The exception was a proposal by the Bush campaign to allow investment of Social Security contributions in the stock market.

The proposal appealed to younger citizens, who have come of political age in a period of relatively ubiquitous stock market activity and who are less confident than their elders in the adequacy of the Social Security system.[13] At the same time, the proposal seemed to cut through the usual New Deal arguments for and against Social Security and the redistributive state.[14] Gore opposed the stock market option, but faced formidable obstacles in making his opposition effective. The arguments he mobilized were necessarily complex and difficult to convey. And his opposition placed him at odds with most of the electorate.

This last point is indicated by figure 4.3. The survey questions underlying the figure took this form:

- Do you personally favor or oppose allowing workers to invest some of their Social Security contributions in the stock market?
- What about George W. Bush/Al Gore? Do you think he favors or opposes allowing workers to invest some of their Social Security contributions in the stock market?

In the figure, opinion and perception are fixed to a −1 (oppose) to +1 (support) range, with respondents who, as the case may be, have no opinion or who cannot make an imputation placed at zero.

All along, as figure 4.3 makes clear, more respondents favored investment than opposed it. All along, Bush's support was more clearly perceived than Gore's opposition. So Bush enjoyed a strategic advantage, and his proposal seems a shrewd gamble. Ironically, Gore might have been well served electorally by remaining in the shadows on the issue.[15] Instead, he chose to make it a centerpiece of his October campaign, to try to explain why the proposal was misconceived.

In doing so, Gore only made matters worse for himself, at least initially. In the week before the first debate, Gore made himself clear to a significantly increased fraction of electorate.[16] Then, the first debate produced a truly dramatic shift for both candidates. About half the total

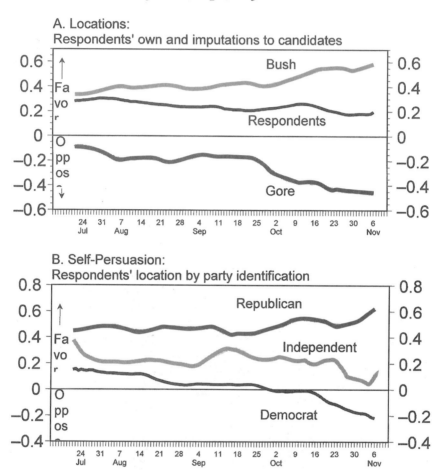

A. Locations:
Respondents' own and imputations to candidates

B. Self-Persuasion:
Respondents' location by party identification

Loess smoothing, bandwidth = 0.20.
Respondents with a major-candidate preference only

Figure 4.3 Social Security and the Stock Market: Locations

campaign shift in Gore perceptions occurred in the five days immediately after this debate. Roughly the same was true for Bush, although,
obviously, the overall range of clarification was smaller. The third
debate widened the perceived Gore–Bush gap yet further.

On balance, all this should have hurt Gore, as it must have made him
seem even more distant than before from the typical voter, both abso-
lutely and relative to Bush. If widening the perceived gap helped prime

the issue for voters, Gore was bound to lose ground. So this too may have contributed to his weaker position in October relative to September.

Not all the news was bad, however. Although the center of opinion on the issue never came over to his side, it did move in his direction. The shift is unmistakable even with the compressed vertical of Panel A. Its magnitude, clarity, and timing come out better with Panel B, which focuses on respondents' own positions and controls party identification. Just as voters got both candidates more clearly in focus, so did they assimilate the new issue to the ongoing battle over the New Deal.

Each party group then moved dramatically toward its own candidate's position. Republicans ended up more clearly than Democrats on their own candidate's side, in itself good news for Bush. But Democrats were more agreed among themselves at the end than at the beginning. Most critically, dynamically speaking, Democrats traversed a greater distance, as on the metric of figure 4.3B their net movement toward Gore was double the Republican movement toward Bush. All movement among Republican identifiers followed immediately on the first debate, and was accomplished before the second one. Among Democrats the first shifts predate the first debate, roughly in keeping with the predebate clarification of Gore's own position. But among Democrats, all early shifts were weak. The truly dramatic movement for Democrats came after the last debate.

Independents marched to their own drummer. For most of the campaign, they simply split the difference between party identification groups and exhibited no net shift of interest. At the very end, however, they moved toward the Democratic position and ended up close to neutral on the issue. These late shifts cannot have hurt Gore; they may have helped him. Relative to September, then, by widening the gap between himself and the median voter, Gore worsened his position. But relative to early October, by dragging the median voter toward himself, he improved his position.

There is much more to say about voters' locations and the locations they imputed to candidates. On the Social Security issue, there is a big story about systematic misperception of Gore, by Democrats in particular. The misperceptions helped Gore rather than hurt him, and by banishing them, he placed his own supporters in a bind. Many resolved the bind by changing their own opinion, as we have just seen.

Although most other issues were not so fertile a field for persuasion or misperception, some were vulnerable to at least some bias or movement. For instance, Gore faced an uphill battle to persuade voters that he favored the death penalty, and Republicans basically never believed him. Beyond the world of political cognition, there is the story of the total issue agenda. Our focus on Social Security and the stock market is justified by its dynamic properties, in voters' perceptions and in their own positions. What we have not demonstrated is how important this was, relative to other issues or to underlying forces like party identification. These are matters for further exploration.[17]

Also ripe for further exploration are processes beyond persuasion. Particularly important is the role of the campaign in shaping the political agenda. Persuasion, on issues at least, is relatively rare. More common, we suspect, is struggle over the agenda, where the challenge is not to change the voter's answer to a given question but to change the very question. This is implicit in our account of clarification in the candidates' positions on Social Security and stock market. Before this clarification, it would have been difficult for the issue to matter much in voters' choice. After clarification, the ground was prepared for this to be a major issue. Was it a major issue in fact?[18]

TOWARD AN INTERPRETATION OF DYNAMICS

Most of the shifts documented in the preceding sections tended to work with preexisting party commitments, rather than cut through them. Of all the considerations, Gore's perceived honesty had the greatest cross-party effect. Republicans and Democrats alike reevaluated him positively in August, and both groups downgraded their evaluations in late September. Republicans downgraded him rather more, however, so the campaign also had the effect of widening preexisting gaps, of reinforcing long-standing partisan bias.

Almost all the net downward reevaluation of Bush came among Democratic identifiers, so here too we see the campaign as reproducing the history of the party system. And, of course, we have shown graphically how on Social Security and the stock market the campaign helped Republicans and Democrats reinterpret a novel issue in familiar terms. In general, persuasion—whether on how to perceive a candidate or on what position to take on an issue—is more likely if it reinforces predisposition, rather than rubs against it.[19]

But this is to say only that persuasion is constrained. It does *not* say that partisan self-persuasion is inevitable, or that persuasion contrary to predisposition is impossible. The existence of constraint by long-term forces does not banish contingency. Gore could have chosen not to emphasize Social Security in the stock market. If it was a mistake for him to emphasize it, at least the last debate gave him a chance to contain the damage. What if that debate had not taken place? This last question also bears on late shifts in perceptions of Bush. Had it not occurred, would his slide among Democrats have accelerated the way it did? Of course, had there been only two debates, campaign strategists would have treated each debate differently. Even so, it is hard to believe that everything about these three debates represents only the unfolding of the inevitable.

Even if subsequent, more refined analyses bear out the intuitions in this chapter, the factors identified so far fall short of accounting for all campaign dynamics of consequence. The accounts built around figures 4.2 and 4.3 address the underlying balance of advantage and disadvantage.[20] Even leaving aside the nominating conventions, there clearly were more dynamics in the campaign than implied in the simple month-by-month comparison. For instance, even though we think of September as a good month for Gore, he trailed Bush several days early in the month. The loess smoothing of figure 4.1 slights these observations, but the facts seem incontrovertible. Did Gore slide in early September simply because the convention impetus played out, or was there active induction by media coverage or by the Bush campaign? Then, what accounts for the mid-September surge, yielding his highest shares of all?[21]

The tracking also alerts us to the speed with which things can change. Even with aggressively smoothed data, we detect phase shifts that seemingly require less than a week. Some critical movements occurred overnight. Sometimes the overnight impulse dissipated, at least in part, and began to do so quickly. But clear turning points and abrupt breaks can be identified. Figure 4.4 makes this point by three-day pooling of days and setting 95 percent confidence bands around the observations. By this construction, seven break points appear, implying a statistically significant difference between consecutive three-day blocks.[22] These are:

- the drop after Bush's acceptance speech,
- the surge before the Democratic Convention,
- the surge after Gore's acceptance speech,
- Gore's mid-September surge,
- the late-September drop that we identify as the strategic turning point of the campaign,
- Gore's surge after the last debate, and
- his drop about one week later.

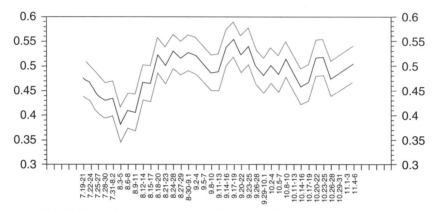

Entry is Gore share plus 95% confidence band for three-day period

Figure 4.4   The Identifiability of Transitions

At this point, political science has nothing resembling a theory of dynamics that can accommodate such abrupt transitions. What little we have for a theory of campaigns has a narrow notion of what counts as a campaign event. Where campaigns have been taken seriously at all, the events that define them have been confined to conventions, debates, and perhaps a handful of major news stories. This is the strategy by Holbrook,[23] for instance. Even more expansive definitions that look to advertising spots and candidate appearances[24] tend to focus on simple whole-campaign magnitudes.

If we expand our inventory of campaign stimuli, we should not expect a simple relationship between the strength of the signal and the magnitude of the response. We are struck by how powerful a response can be invoked by modest induction; this will almost certainly be a conclusion from full analysis of Gore's critical late-September downturn. In general, there seems to be slippage between the intention and the act, and yet when the link is made, action can change suddenly. And for some fraction of the electorate, intention may reflect quite superficial forces, the latest blast of positive or negative coverage. The fraction may not be large and probably shrinks over the course of the campaign.[25] But if these voters respond to a common stimulus—common precisely because, positive or negative valence aside, it is contentless?—they can be decisive at the margin.

This may help us understand why candidates worry so much about their late-stage itineraries. It also suggests that we take certain mass-audience television programs seriously as potential campaign events. Taking such phenomena seriously will deepen our understanding of forces we already know to be important, such as party identification. But taking them seriously might also teach us a little humility in the face of the contingency in things.

NOTES

1. The typical campaign sees the front-runner ahead by nearly twenty points on Labor Day. The lead is eventually cut in half, but this only implies that the final margin is a comfortable ten points. Only twice before, 1948 and 1960, did the Labor Day front-runner lose the election. Where the Labor Day front-runner wins, he does not as a rule lose the lead in the interim. An exception seems to be 1980, where the lead changed several times but the Labor Day front-runner (Ronald Reagan) won. See James E. Campbell, *The American Campaign: US Presidential Campaigns and the National Vote* (College Station: Texas A&M Press, 2000); see also Christopher Wlezien, "On Forecasting the Presidential Vote," *PS: Political Science and Politics* 34 (2001): 25–31.

2. Daily updates were available at PollingReport.com, and by early October each day brought several readings from alternative sources. By our count from PollingReport.com, polls appeared with the following frequency, averaged by month: August, 1.1 per day; September, 2.5 per day; October, 4.8 per day; and November (first week), 6.8 per day. Cable News Network (CNN), *USA Today,* and Gallup began daily tracking on September 6 and by the end at least four other survey houses were reporting daily numbers.

3. Special mention must be made of Mary McIntosh and Chris Adasiewicz at PSRA, without whom the whole enterprise would have foundered.

4. In the presidential primary season, the national sample was supplemented by oversamples in key primary electorates. At various points along the way, panel reinterviews were also conducted. Some of these were retrospections on the election just concluded, including panel interviews conducted after November 7. Some panels bracketed key campaign events, the nominating conventions, and presidential debates.

5. The logic of the design is outlined in Richard Johnston and Henry E. Brady, "The Rolling Cross-Section Design," *Electoral Studies* (forthcoming).

6. The start date for the plot reflects the timing of changes to the Annenberg questionnaire, as only on July 17 did we set in place a four-candidate query. The data in this chapter are screened only for vote intention and are not weighted. We are struck that the late-campaign Gore share of our respondents' two-party intentions is almost exactly the share he ultimately received. All attempts to screen for interest or other such purported indicators of "likely vote" only worsen the predictive value of late samples, much as Irving Crespi found in *Pre-Election Polling: Sources of Accuracy and Error* (New York: Russell Sage Foundation, 1988).

7. Our tracking from the beginning of the year with a two-candidate question

indicates that Gore gained on Bush over the primary season, then dissipated those gains from April to July.

8. Thomas M. Holbrook, *Do Campaigns Matter?* (Thousand Oaks, Calif.: Sage, 1996).

9. Larry M. Bartels and John Zaller, "Presidential Vote Models: A Recount," *PS: Political Science and Politics* 34 (2001): 9–20.

10. This is consistent for the whole convention sequence with the interpretation in Holbrook, *Do Campaigns Matter?*

11. For a description of the battery and a justification of its content and structure, see Donald R. Kinder, "Presidential Traits," Pilot Study Report to the 1984 NES Planning Committee and the NES Board (Ann Arbor: University of Michigan, 1983).

12. Note that each panel in figure 4.2 has a 0.4 point range, but each spans a different section of the overall range of -1 to +1.

13. Among our respondents, the age gradient in support for this proposal is quite steep.

14. Before October, for example, there was almost no relationship between respondents' liberal/conservative self-placement and their support for the stock market option.

15. He did attempt to deflect potential damage by supporting a voluntary contribution scheme, where the existing structure of premiums and funding is preserved.

16. The daily tracking suggests a discontinuity between September 27 and 28. Note that Gore had become slightly more clear in voters' minds in early August as well. This occurred before the Democratic convention and so is something of a mystery.

17. For a start, see Michael G. Hagen, Richard Johnston, and Kathleen Hall Jamieson, "Dynamics of the 2000 Presidential Campaign: Evidence from the Annenberg Study," paper presented at the annual conference of the American Association for Public Opinion Research, Montreal, Quebec, May 17–20, 2001.

18. A more refined but still preliminary analysis suggests that the issue did indeed gain power. See Hagen, Johnston, and Jamieson, "Dynamics of the 2000 Presidential Campaign," Table 1.

19. This is a standard proposition in the social and cognitive psychology literatures as well as in electoral studies, dating at least as far back as Bernard Berelson, Paul F. Lazarsfeld, and William N. McPhee, *Voting* (Chicago: University of Chicago Press, 1954), and as far forward as Shanto Iyengar and Donald R. Kinder, *News That Matters: Television and American Opinion* (Chicago: University of Chicago Press, 1995).

20. "Underlying," that is, on the time scale of weeks or, at most, months.

21. We mention the following only in a footnote, the better to underscore our diffidence. It is a fact that Gore's mid-September surge follows his appearance on the Oprah Winfrey show. There is also a downward spike, September 20–22, that follows Bush's appearance on the same program with a one-day lag. Could appearance on an entertainment-oriented interview show be the national-audience good-news equivalent of a candidate appearance in a state?

22. If we pool three-day blocks around some other apparent discontinuities, we

would identify still more critical abrupt shifts. In general, the time paths and magnitude of short-term shifts also make us wonder if the concerns expressed in John Zaller, "Assessing the Statistical Power of Election Studies to Detect Communication Effects in Political Campaigns," *Electoral Studies* (forthcoming), are exaggerated.

23. Holbrook, *Do Campaigns Matter?*

24. Daron R. Shaw, "The Effect of TV Ads and Candidate Appearances on Statewide Presidential Votes, 1988–96," *American Political Science Review* 93 (1999): 345–361.

25. This certainly seems to be the implication of Christopher Wlezien and Robert S. Erikson, "The Timeline of Presidential Election Campaigns," unpublished, 2000. See especially their Figure 6.

GOVERNMENTAL INSTITUTIONS

5

The Presidential Transition into a Fifty-Fifty Government, and Beyond

Charles O. Jones, University of Wisconsin at Madison

Writing in the *Washington Post*, Robert J. Samuelson summarized the 2000 presidential election this way: "No self-respecting screenwriter would have submitted this election script. It is too contrived. The antagonists . . . are too self-absorbed and self-interested. There are no heroes."[1] It is a decent paraphrase of Samuelson's observation to state: "No self-respecting scholar would have submitted this election forecast. It is too improbable." Political scientists modeling the election in advance were surely inclined to agree. To a person, they forecast a win for Al Gore, ranging from 52.8 percent to 60.3 percent of the popular vote.[2] It is true, of course, that George W. Bush won so narrowly as to raise doubts about his legitimacy. But he was not supposed to win at all, narrowly or otherwise.

The 2000 national election produced a government without precedent in modern history, perhaps ever. The new president won a tie in quadruple overtime, with the U.S. Supreme Court calling time. The House Republican majority narrowed to just five seats, nine seats more than the Democrats. A fifty-fifty split in the Senate forced the Republicans into a power-sharing agreement with the Democrats there. Republicans won nominal control of all three elected branches for the first time since 1953, but with limited political capital and full responsibility. On the positive side for President Bush, few election analysts were moved to speak of a "mandate," that inapt concept as applied to

93

American politics. Accordingly, expectations were low, with gridlock forecast by many.

However "contrived" or "improbable," the script prepared by the voters had to be followed by ordinary politicians, not heroes, with improvisation required for the pauses in dialogue. The prospective presidents-elect worked within limited degrees of freedom toward an uncertain outcome. For not only was it doubtful who would win, but victory itself raised serious issues for governing. Political conditions demanded more exacting preparations than usual, yet the time for unfettered attention to planning was cut in half. And when it was finally over, there would be no exception made for the strains of the farfetched aftermath. The fifty-fifty president would still be held responsible for that fifty-fifty government.

THE PERMANENT CAMPAIGN EVOLVES

The traditional passages to the presidency are straightforward: from announced candidate to party nominee to president-elect to president, and thus from campaigning roles to governing roles. The principal transformation occurs the day after the election. "A candidate the day before, the winner is president-elect the day after. 'It's like flicking a light switch. The next day, it's different.'"[3] In 2000, however, it was even more different. Election day did not transform one candidate into the president-elect. Recounts, contests, court challenges, and competition for media coverage characterized this new phase instead. New passages to the presidency were introduced. Gore and Bush had to plan ahead while enhancing and protecting their claims to victory.

The first new passage was that of "president-elect in waiting." Each candidate had a credible basis for expecting a win; yet neither could legitimately declare victory. One can only imagine the anxiety experienced by both camps after months of intense campaigning.

The second postelection passage was experienced only by Bush. Following his certification on November 26 by Katherine Harris, the Florida secretary of state, Bush became the "president-elect without full portfolio." Being declared the winner in Florida put him just barely over the top in the Electoral College count—271. Now he could plan more actively to organize his presidency. Gore, however, exercised his option under Florida law to contest certification. Therefore, the General Services Administration would not authorize funds or office space for the Bush transition team.

Gore's role during this time must have been even more anxiety-ridden. The Harris certification of Bush had put Gore at a substantial disadvantage. As "president-elect in waiting," November 8–26, he was on a par with Bush. With certification, Bush took a giant step forward. Gore was still "in waiting," now for success in the courts. It was difficult under the circumstances for him to concentrate on transition planning. Legal maneuvering took precedence, with Gore assuming active, behind-the-scenes direction of the effort. First things were bound to be first: the Gore team needed to find the votes to overcome Bush's slight lead or there would be no transition.

Upon learning that the networks had withdrawn their call of Florida for Bush in the early morning hours of November 8, Gore's campaign director, William Daley, declared: "The campaign continues." Little did Daley know at that time that his declaration would become prophecy. The permanent campaign invaded the crucial period of building an administration. In the past, election day was thought to be the end of the campaign. In describing John F. Kennedy's transition, Richard E. Neustadt observed that: "Part of the brilliance was that those people could not wait to start governing. They were so glad the campaign was over."[4] Now campaigning is a part of governing, a development substantially intensified during the Clinton presidency. We are in an "era of the permanent campaign" in which "the process of campaigning and the process of governing have lost their distinctiveness."[5]

The irresolution on November 7 ensured that campaigning would continue. The race essentially ended in a tie nationally in the popular vote and was so close in the Electoral College that Florida's electors were decisive. But Florida voters also split fifty-fifty. A recount was automatic and a contest by the loser following certification was likely. Given extensive media coverage of the counts and the courts, both candidate organizations had to remain in a campaign mode.

Opinion polls came to be an important measure of success, as they do during an election campaign. Especially important were tests of the public's patience after the Florida certification. Bush gained an initial advantage in these polls. Should Gore concede? Yes: 60 percent (ABC News/*Washington Post*), 56 percent (CNN–*USA Today*–Gallup), 49 percent (NBC News). Has Bush won the presidency? Yes: 61 percent (NBC News).[6] A Mason-Dixon poll in late November showed that 62 percent of voters accepted Bush as the winner in Florida, including 24 percent of those who voted for Gore.[7]

Understandably, these results prompted Gore to intensify his efforts to justify his legal actions with several appearances on television in the week following the Florida certification. The Bush forces responded, mostly with on-camera briefings on the work of forming a presidency. In reflecting on the Clinton presidency, I concluded: "Given that campaigning carries over into governing, readiness must begin as early as possible."[8] I had not anticipated that campaigning would invade the transition period.

Rather, I was suggesting the need for the president-elect to prepare for constant campaigning once in office, for example, by integrating second-generation political consultants (those prepared to conduct policy as well as electoral campaigns) into the White House staff in a manner so as not to interfere with regular staff operations. As it was, however, the transition period in 2000 featured an overlay of nonstop campaigning, with campaign staff working alongside those organizing the new presidency. Campaign directors, political consultants, pollsters, and press liaison personnel did not go away; rather, their numbers were supplemented by legions of lawyers, former cabinet and White House officials, members of Congress, and sitting governors.

One of the more arresting features of the Florida recount phase was the sequence of political trumps through court and legislative actions (including the potential involvement of Congress). Consider that a *Republican* Secretary of State (Katherine Harris) had authority to certify Bush as the winner. A Florida Supreme Court, mostly appointed by *Democratic* governors, extended the deadline for certification, directed the Secretary of State to accept hand-counted ballots, and then ordered a count of so-called undervotes in heavily *Democratic* counties. A *Republican*-controlled state legislature called for a special session to appoint electors (an action then to be signed by the Florida governor, a brother of the candidate). A U.S. Supreme Court, mostly appointed by *Republican* presidents, vacated the Florida Supreme Court's first order and then halted the recount authorized by its later decision.

Finally, had it come to that, the choice between contested Florida electors would have had to be made by the U.S. House and Senate sitting separately, with the *Republicans* in a majority in the House and a tie in the Senate likely broken in favor of the *Democrats* by one of the presidential candidates (Gore) sitting as President of the Senate. And the ultimate choice of electors, by the rules governing this situation, would be those officially certified by the signature of the Florida Governor, that same brother of one of the candidates (Bush). There were other checkmates favoring the *Democrats* within the lower courts in Florida, but the point has been made.

It was within this political context, real and prospective, that the transition advanced. Virtually every facet of this extraordinary election decreed that the president-elect would have to prepare a left- or right-centrist, cross-partisan presidency. Achieving this goal during the pseudotransition period (i.e., before a definitive conclusion in Florida) was made more difficult by the serial cross-checking noted above. Furthermore, the very nature of legal challenges during this time moved the issues in a more partisan direction. By the very nature of their craft, lawyers harden the case to be made, thus moving away from what is by definition required to govern with a fifty-fifty result throughout the elected government.

DOES A TIE MEAN GRIDLOCK?

Elsewhere I have argued that the separated system can enhance the speculative imagination so essential for democratic lawmaking.[9] Separated institutions cultivate and safeguard competitive speculation, which is itself fostered by leeway. My unconventional view is that a fifty-fifty government has the potential of offering substantial leeway. Both political parties are at even strength and therefore may be motivated to generate serious policy proposals. A president can benefit from these efforts in forging cross-partisan coalitions. The challenge for a president-elect under these circumstances is to realize this potential, beginning with the transition and extending to his first days and weeks in office.

The more conventional gridlock scenario for a fifty-fifty government is easily portrayed and frequently peddled. Yet it underestimates the political savvy, professional status, and career motivations of elected officials. Presidents like to propose; legislators like to legislate; both sets like to take credit and avoid blame. More likely, therefore, is a scenario in which politicians design governing strategies for taking advantage of the latitude offered by an even split. What does that mean? Simply this: Equal strength accords each party the power to prevent purely partisan advantages for the other party. Strength in numbers or status encourages development and promotion of competing policy proposals (copartisanship); the prospect of stalemate fosters interparty agreements (cross-partisanship). Neither party gains with stalemate; both may profit from legislative production.

Contrast the fifty-fifty case with that of overwhelming partisan advantages, as with President Lyndon B. Johnson and the 89th Congress, in which Democrats had two-thirds majorities. Such conditions tend to thwart widespread participation in all phases of lawmaking. The minority party may well cultivate a mentality of futility, retreating to service functions for survival as elected representatives. The majority party may acquiesce to presidential leadership (e.g., the New Deal and Great Society). The ordinary benefits of the separated system are lost. So, in fact, evenly divided government (as in 2001) or split-party government in various forms (as experienced most of the time after 1945) can activate the speculative imagination, thus promoting the creative tension that is the energy of the democratic lawmaking process.

None of this is to suggest that the president forgo leadership and accede to the proposals offered by the other party due to its strength in Congress. It suggests, instead, that there are advantages for the president in a constructively active and motivated opposition. As used here, leeway is a creatively augmenting concept. It allows a greater margin for designing policy and enacting law. The president proposes, and so do members of Congress. The very essence of representation as a governing principle is that interests are actively revealed and their preferences displayed.

Presidents are assumed to do well if the best laws are enacted and implemented. The challenge then is for a president in a split-party or fifty-fifty government to take full advantage of the competitive spirit and shared accountability of each party. This effort by the president will be the measure of effectiveness in leadership, sensitive as it must be to what the margins are, what is and is not a positive contribution, and when to strike the bargain. As an aside, note that President Bill Clinton's major successes in Congress came not in the first two years when he had Democratic majorities but in 1996 and 1997 when Republicans held majorities in both houses of Congress.[10]

Among the greatest hazards for a president-elect in meeting these challenges are the expectations of those I have labeled the "unitarians," that is, those who favor a presidential government with party responsibility.

> For the unitarian, the best possible election result is that in which one political party wins the White House and majority control of both houses of Congress. The party is then expected to display unity on policy issues and to produce a record for which it can be held responsible at the next election. Political unitarians are unhappy with our arrangement of disconnected elections that can produce split-party government. At root, the unitarians disagree with the separation of powers principle of coequal branches.[11]

The *mandate* is central to the unitarian perspective. As party leader, the president is charged with putting it into effect. So dominant is the motif of the mandate that it was even used by some in writing about the 2000 presidential election in which the winner lost the popular vote to the loser and won a five-vote victory in the Electoral College in quadruple overtime. How can this emphasis be explained? Possibly by the several conditions advancing it: for example, media reporting on the presidential campaign and election as a horse race, the quadrennial national party convention serving primarily to nominate a presidential candidate, the singularity of the presidential race over the election of 435 representatives and a third of the Senate, and the ceremony and celebration of a new leader at the inaugural.

As one journalist explained to me: "If elections aren't a mandate for something, then what do they mean?"[12] Robert A. Dahl supplied the answer: An election "confers the legitimate authority, right, and opportunity on a president to try to gain the adoption by constitutional means of the policies the president supports."[13]

The president-centric perspective can have effects on those preparing to govern, perhaps even to the extent of overreaching. Neustadt has described the election of a new president this way: "Everywhere there is a sense of a page turning, a new chapter in the country's history, a new chance too. And, with it, irresistibly, there comes the sense, 'they' couldn't, wouldn't, didn't, but 'we' will."[14] Neustadt detected hazards for the transition in this situation, notably "ignorance," "haste," and "hubris."

> In advising on presidential transitions, risks for the adviser can be summarized as ignorance compounded by inhibitions and haste. While *ignorance* can mean not knowing, it can also mean not comprehending what in some sense one may know. . . .
>
> Haste is a hazard for the objects of advice—for Presidents-elect and their immediate associates—no less than for would-be advisers . . . [and] haste is unavoidable. So is hubris, at least in the form of arrogance and innocence, combined. . . . The arrogance, at best, consists of thinking that "we won, so we can, while they didn't and couldn't," amplified by almost certain overestimation of the Presidency's potency.
>
> From any other office in our political system, it looks comparatively strong, much stronger than it does from inside. Thus, those about to climb inside for the first time are almost bound to overestimate the power that will soon be theirs. In that consists their innocence.[15]

Separationist realities intrude rather soon after the inauguration as presidents and their aides settle into the presidency. Grand ambitions are soon ratcheted down to suit political circumstances of power sharing within the permanent government. A core reality of the postwar period is that seldom can presidents expect to govern with a purely partisan strategy. Seven of the ten presidents during this time (Truman, Eisenhower, Nixon, Ford, Reagan, George H. W. Bush, and Clinton) served with Congresses of the other party (one house or both). Presidents-elect in six of the fourteen elections (Truman, Kennedy, Nixon, Clinton twice, and George W. Bush) did not receive a majority of the popular vote. Two others (Carter and Reagan, first term) barely received a majority (50.1 percent and 50.7 percent, respectively).

This record clearly indicates that most presidents have to develop co-, cross-, and bipartisan strategies for governing. In fact, campaigning may be expected to continue into governing. Ordinarily, therefore, presidents-elect are well advised to prepare their presidencies during the transition and beyond to build public support so as to enhance status in working across party lines. That surely was the consequence of the 2000 election. Still, every president faces the challenge of managing the high expectations associated with an enduring unitarian perspective on the presidency.

GEORGE W. BUSH AND ALBERT A. GORE JR.: THE MODEL TRANSITION CANDIDATES

There have been five open presidential races in the post–World War II era: 1952, 1960, 1968, 1988, and 2000. In the four most recent cases, sitting vice presidents were candidates—Nixon, 1960; Humphrey, 1968; Bush, 1988; and Gore, 2000.[16] Given their status in the previous administration, one might expect that they would be familiar with the problems and mechanics of a presidential transition.[17] In three of these races, the opposing candidates too had Washington experience or connections such as to suggest an orderly transition—Kennedy, 1960; Nixon, 1968; and Bush, 2000.

Of these five sets of candidates in open races, Gore and Bush were among the more fully prepared, though for different reasons and with contrasting skills that were revealing of their likely presidential styles.[18] Gore had extensive governmental service in Washington, as had his father before him. In 1976, Gore was elected from Tennessee to the U.S. House of Representatives, where he served four terms. He was elected to the U.S. Senate in 1984 and reelected in 1990. He ran unsuccessfully for his party's presidential nomination in 1988. It was thought that he might seek the nomination again in 1992, but the early strength of President Bush convinced him to forgo the race. Clinton then chose him as his running mate in 1992.

During his eight years of service as vice president, Gore was heavily involved in the reinventing government exercise, thus acquainting him with organizational issues of the national government. He was also very much a partner of Clinton, perhaps to a greater extent than any vice president. Here then was a presidential candidate who had been in elected public office in Washington for twenty-four years. He had been in place to observe the transitions of Carter, Reagan, and George Bush and was actively involved in the transition of Clinton.

By reason of this experience, Gore might have been expected to have a smooth transition—one mostly "by the book." But there were complications, notably those associated with a serving vice president succeeding his president. There are not many such cases in history—four total (John Adams, Thomas Jefferson, Martin Van Buren, and George Bush) and just one (Bush) since 1836. The Reagan-to-Bush case was the most relevant for Gore. An "understudy" president has the special problem of separating himself from his predecessor without seeming to be turning his back on an administration of which he was a part.[19] It is a particular problem if the predecessor was a popular president as measured by the job approval ratings.

Among other effects, many political appointees of the previous administration may well expect to be held over, thus either reducing the president-elect's options or creating resentments. Further complicating the matter is the reality that the pool of experienced personnel is naturally dominated by those presently holding positions in the outgoing administration. Paul C. Light observed that "Gore can't afford to be the president of Clinton holdovers. It's not a sustainable political position."[20] Perhaps so. And yet there is only so much talent for and experience in governing that is available and willing to serve, thereby limiting the president-elect's choices.

George W. Bush could not match Gore's Washington-based experience. But he also had a number of advantages for conducting an effective transition. He was serving his second four-year term as Governor of Texas, the second most populated state. He had, therefore, managed a transition into an important elected office, having defeated a popular incumbent Democratic governor in 1994 and subsequently forming his governing team. Equally important was the fact that his father had served as president, 1989–1993, and previously held numerous major posts in government. As a result, Bush had a substantial pool of experienced hands available for advising him in regard to building a government. Perhaps most notable among these was his running mate, Richard B. Cheney, who had served as White House Chief of Staff, a Representative from Wyoming, House Minority Whip, and Secretary of Defense.

Unlike Cheney, many other senior officials in the previous Bush, Reagan, and Ford administrations were reluctant themselves to return to government. But they were willing to provide counsel in regard to personnel, policy, and political matters. A second source for experienced appointments lay in the many Republican governors, several of whom had urged Bush to run. These governors provided advice and political support during the campaign, and some were even active during the five-week period following the election. Again, not all were seeking appointments, but they represented vast experience in government and in administering federal programs at the state level.

On the less positive side, the governing experience of officials in previous Republican administrations was eight or more years in the past. Much had changed in policy and politics in that time. Thus, for example, huge deficits were transformed into real and prospective surpluses. Deficits dominated policymaking for nearly two decades, essentially defining a generation of politics in which both political parties concentrated on budget management. Surpluses encourage more traditional party stances—Democrats for government programs, Republicans for tax cuts.

It is also the case that state experience is only marginally transferable to Washington. Governing a large state is more relevant to managing the presidency than governing a small state, but each state is exceptional. For example, Governor Bush was heralded as working well with Democrats in the Texas state legislature. That experience no doubt contributed to his favorable attitude toward cross-party politics. But Texas Democrats are not congressional Democrats, as Bush's father could attest. Accordingly, President Bush would have to adapt his cross-party inclinations to a substantially more professional and career-oriented Congress.

It is also the case that a governor's experience in foreign policy is typically limited to parochial trade issues. Yet there are few more important policy spheres for a new administration. Presidents-elect who have served as governors some distance from Washington typically need help. In Bush's case, he had available an unusually experienced coterie of persons with distinguished records of service in foreign and national security policy. Personally, however, he had no more background than any of the other recent governors serving as president—Carter, Reagan, or Clinton.

As it happened, having two well-prepared candidates by reason of experience and close associates was critically important in 2000. The delay in reaching a definitive choice for president seriously reduced the time for forming a new administration. However important it was in the past to "hit the ground running," it was vital in 2001. The probability was high that both Gore and Bush could meet this test.[21]

THE BUSH TRANSITION

The normal, formal transition period extends from the day after the election to the inaugural on January 20. Thus, a new president has approximately ten weeks to create a new administration. He is expected during this time to nominate his cabinet and other high-profile positions; to select his White House staff; to establish a theme and direction for his presidency; to identify his policy priorities; and, if he is from out of town, to introduce himself to the Washington establishment. Attaining those goals in the time allotted, while dismantling a huge campaign apparatus, is a challenging assignment under the best of circumstances. In the case of George W. Bush, however, all of this had to be accomplished in thirty-eight days, approximately half the normal time available to a new president-elect. For it was not until December 13 that Gore conceded defeat, following the U.S. Supreme Court's decision that effectively halted the recount of votes in Florida.

Sensibly, the Bush team did not wait for the Gore concession to act on the transition. The phases of its activities more or less suited the new passages noted earlier: from president-elect in waiting (November 8–26) to president-elect without full portfolio (November 26–December 13) to president-elect (December 13–January 20) to president (January 20 forward). During the first passage, the Bush forces made initial preparations. Key decisions regarding the management of the transition and some appointments were confirmed during the second passage. The plans were implemented during the third phase, with full attention to the three basic elements of a transition: people, precepts, and policies. And many confirmations and lesser appointments carried over beyond January 20.

After the election, the Bush team postured as the incoming administration. It had the slight advantage of a small but persistent margin in the series of Florida counts. Planning proceeded in Austin, Texas, where Bush was still serving as governor. Meanwhile in Florida, the Bush lawyers, campaign staff, and various elected officials from the state houses and Congress managed the legal and public opinion aspects of the recount. Former Secretary of State James A. Baker III served as the spokesperson for the Bush effort in Florida. Bush had a low profile, limiting himself to occasional statements.

Just three days after the election, Bush held a much-publicized meeting of "a potential administration." Cameras were invited in as Bush let it be known that Cheney would head the transition and that Andrew Card (Secretary of Transportation in the earlier Bush administration) would serve as White House Chief of Staff. Bush stated: "I think . . . the country needs to know—that this administration will be ready to assume office and be prepared to lead. I think it's up to us to prepare the groundwork for an administration that will be ready to function on Day One."[22] Karl Rove, a top Bush political adviser, observed: "The process ought to move forward. We cannot stop and wait until the last ballot struggles in."[23] No potential cabinet secretaries were present at this early meeting; rather, those attending were from the campaign policy team—reinforcing the notion that the meeting was staged primarily for the press.

Not unexpectedly, the Gore team criticized this early show of intentions as presumptuous, even arrogant. However, it was engaged in a highly sensitive challenge to the automatic recount in Florida that reduced Bush's lead but did not erase it. Their preoccupation was with the complexities involved as well as the extent to which Democrats would support a prolonged effort, particularly if that resulted in court action. "A source close to both Gore and congressional Democrats said, 'A lot of them now feel Gore actually did win it. If we can get there in a way that doesn't poison the well, then fine. If not, they expect him to be a statesman.'"[24]

However small the Bush lead in Florida (and it was minuscule), it enabled forward thinking and ensured party support. The more immediate challenge for the Gore team was to gain similar advantages. For Gore, public talk of transition planning had to be postponed, though planning itself proceeded under the direction of Roy Neel, a former Gore aide.[25] Sensitive to the public's patience with delays and possible erosion of Democratic support, Gore, in a brief televised address on November 15, invited Bush to join him in accepting the results of the manual recounts, possibly in all sixty-seven counties. Gore also proposed rejecting any further legal actions by both sides and that the two candidates meet "to improve the tone of our dialogue." Caught by surprise, the Bush team nevertheless recognized Gore's offer for the political move it was and refused it.[26]

The Bush team expected Secretary of State Katherine Harris of Florida to certify its win on November 18, following the count of the remaining overseas absentee ballots. At the last minute, however, the Florida Supreme Court enjoined a decision by Secretary Harris pending its review of challenges by the Gore team. The following Tuesday, November 21, the Florida Supreme Court ruled that manual recounts in three counties had to be included in the final tally with the counting itself to be concluded by 5 P.M. on November 26. Elated, Gore again spoke to the nation, repeating some of what he had earlier offered to Bush but, as well, stating that it was time for both camps to concentrate on transition planning.

The Bush response to the Florida Supreme Court decision was an appeal to the U.S. Supreme Court to halt the count, described in the petition as "selective, capricious and standardless" and taking place in "a handful of unrepresentative Florida counties."[27] Of the three counties authorized by the court to conduct manual recounts, one completed its count in that time, one abandoned the effort, and one was unable to finish by 5 P.M. on Sunday. Secretary Harris, flanked by the two other members of the Elections Canvassing Commission, certified George W. Bush as the winner of Florida's twenty-five electoral votes. The Gore forces immediately exercised their right under Florida law to contest the certification.

The effect of the contested certification was to provide Bush with a significant strategic advantage. He could now justifiably proceed apace with transition organizational decisions and posture more confidently as the president-elect. To fully comprehend the advantage then enjoyed by Bush, one only need ponder what certification would have done for Gore at that point. Another measure of the advantage gained by certification, however tentative, was the press speculation about who would serve on the White House staff and in the cabinet. There was a great deal of conjecturing about Bush's choices, very little about Gore's. In fact, Gore sought to counter this attention by launching a "public relations offensive . . . asserting in a series of television appearances that he believes he won Florida's 25 electoral votes."[28]

A confident and business-like attitude was projected by the Bush team after November 26. Cheney, recently recovered from a heart attack, was confirmed as chair of the transition, as were Card as White House Chief of Staff and Clay Johnson as transition director. The General Services Administration would not authorize either transition funds or office space to Bush because of the contested ballot count in Florida. Using privately raised funds, the transition directors set up an interim office in McLean, Virginia. Meanwhile, President Clinton created a transition council headed by his Chief of Staff John Podesta, who acted as the chief liaison person for the Bush team in communicating with the Clinton White House. Intelligence briefings were arranged for Bush, and Attorney General Janet Reno announced that the Department of Justice was prepared to conduct background checks on prospective appointees for both Bush and Gore. At long last, the transition was underway even as the nation awaited the definitive choice of president.

Other confidence-building actions by the Bush team (for itself and the public) included a meeting with Colin Powell as a confirming signal of his front-runner status as Secretary of State, meetings with governors and congressional Republicans to discuss legislative priorities, opening of the interim transition headquarters in Virginia, and frequent reiteration of the need, even the responsibility, to move ahead with the transition. This activity, however, barely masked the impatience and frustration of the Bush staff in Florida and Austin.

Few of the campaign staff were assigned to the transition, many more were at work in Florida, and the largest number had to wait for a definitive conclusion to the election. As one report indicated: "Uncertainty permeates the nascent Bush administration. Publicly, the Bush campaign says it is proceeding with a transition, but this is easier said than done."[29] Among other concerns were the fears among junior staff that their future jobs might be threatened by an unwitting misstep during this strange time. As one observed: "You don't want to do anything unorthodox or unauthorized because it can come back and bite you."[30]

Meanwhile, intricate legal and political actions were occurring in Florida and Washington. In the political arena, leaders of the Republican-controlled Florida legislature began a move for a special session to authorize Bush electors. On the judicial front, a breathtaking series of actions filled a ten-day period. In order, the U.S. Supreme Court nullified the Florida Supreme Court's order of November 21, pending further explanation of its decision; Circuit Judge N. Sanders Sauls of Leon County rejected Gore's request for a manual recount of so-called "undervotes"; the Florida Supreme Court defied most expectations and ordered the manual recount to resume, also awarding votes to Gore that earlier were denied by Secretary Harris; the U.S. Supreme Court ordered an immediate halt to the manual recount, pending its review on appeal; and on December 12, the U.S. Supreme Court reversed the order of the Florida Supreme Court. It remained only for Gore to concede defeat, which he did the following day.

"For the sake of our unity of the people and the strength of our democracy, I offer my concession." Thus did Gore authenticate a Bush presidency. "Neither he nor I anticipated this long and difficult road. Certainly neither of us wanted it to happen. Yet it came, and now it has ended, resolved, as it must be resolved, through the honored institutions of our democracy."[31] Bush acknowledged that he had received a "gracious call from the vice president." He stated that the two had agreed to meet in Washington, "and we agreed to do our best to heal our country after this hard-fought contest."[32]

MAKING A TRANSITION

At long last, the Bush transition could proceed for real—no more distractions to divert the staff and raise doubts about the legitimacy of his planning. Major White House staff appointments were already in place, but these appointments could now be confirmed: Andrew Card as Chief of Staff, Ari Fleisher as Press Secretary, Karen Hughes as Counselor, and Alberto Gonzales as Counsel. Later, Karl Rove was chosen as the Assistant for Political Affairs and Mitchell Daniels the Director of the Office of Management and Budget.

Press attention naturally focused on the cabinet. In recent cases of a party shift, the president-elect typically made his first nominations the second week in December, completing the choice of cabinet secretaries by Christmas. President-elect Bush had to act much more swiftly, and he did. Of course, he had the five weeks of the Florida vote count to consider potential nominees. Yet he could not so openly interview candidates or benefit from a public vetting of names. And any obvious moves to build a cabinet would be criticized as brash, even arrogant.

C. Boyden Gray, former Counsel to the first President Bush, summarized the appointment process as "innocent until nominated."[33] No one can quite know in advance what will turn up in the background checks of a nominee by the Federal Bureau of Investigation, in financial disclosure forms, in the questioning in confirmation hearings before Senate committees, or in investigations by the media and other groups. Based on a Brookings Institution survey of prospective appointees, Paul C. Light observed that "the appointment process itself has been the most significant barrier" to convincing quality executives to enter government service.[34] On the one hand, it was remarkable, therefore, that Bush was successful in attracting experienced individuals to the cabinet in a short period of time. On the other hand, he was no more successful than other recent presidents in swiftly appointing subcabinet positions, as shown by the Brookings project on appointments.[35]

The first appointment had been signaled well in advance—even early in the campaign. Colin Powell, former National Security Adviser and Chair of the Joint Chiefs of Staff, had hinted a willingness to serve in the cabinet when he declined to run as a vice presidential candidate with Bush. And he delivered a prime address at the Republican National Convention. His appointment as Secretary of State was announced on December 16, just three days after Gore's concession. The following day Bush revealed another unsurprising choice, Condoleezza Rice as National Security Adviser. Over the next seventeen days, Bush completed his cabinet secretarial appointments. It was the most rapid designation of these posts following final declaration of the winner in recent times—perhaps ever (see table 5.1).

Linda Chavez withdrew her name from consideration on January 9 when it was revealed that she had sheltered an illegal alien from Guatemala. Bush acted swiftly. Two days later, he nominated Elaine Lan Chao for the Labor post. Chao was a fellow at the Heritage Foundation and had served previously as President of the United Way, Director of the Peace Corps, Deputy Secretary of the Department of Transportation, and Chairman of the Federal Maritime Commission.

There are several interesting characteristics of this group. Perhaps most impressive is their governmental executive experience—thirteen of the fifteen qualify (including three governors and three cabinet secretaries). Only Donald L. Evans and Spencer Abraham lacked such experience; the former was a CEO who had chaired the Bush–Cheney campaign, while the latter formerly chaired the Michigan Republican Party. Here is a breakdown of the types of service and occupation:

Federal service: 7
Law: 7
State service: 5
Business: 5
Legislative service: 5
Education, charitable, think tank: 4
Local service: 3

The group was unquestionably conservative—hardly surprising. One Democrat was included: Norman Y. Mineta, who was serving in President Clinton's cabinet as Secretary of Commerce. There was somewhat more representation of state and local service than usual; somewhat less

Table 5.1   Cabinet Appointments to the Bush Administration

December 16:
State: Colin L. Powell (Chairman, America's Promise–The Alliance for Youth; former Chairman Joint Chiefs of Staff, National Security Adviser)

December 20:
Agriculture: Ann M. Veneman (Secretary, California Department of Food and Agriculture; former Deputy Secretary, U.S. Department of Agriculture)
Commerce: Donald L. Evans (Chairman, Bush–Cheney 2000; Chairman and CEO, Tom Brown, Inc., an oil exploration company)
Housing and Urban Development: Mel Martinez (Chairman, Orange County Florida; former President, Orlando Utilities Commission, and Chairman, Orlando Housing Authority)
Treasury: Paul H. O'Neill (Chairman, Alcoa; former Deputy Director, Office of Management and Budget)

December 22:
Justice: John Ashcroft (former Missouri Senator, Governor, and Attorney General)
Environmental Protection Agency: Christine Todd Whitman (New Jersey Governor; former President of New Jersey Board of Public Utilities)

December 28:
Defense: Donald H. Rumsfeld (CEO, General Instrument Corporation; former Secretary of Defense, White House Chief of Staff, NATO Ambassador, Director of OEO, and Member of the House of Representatives)

December 29:
Education: Rod Paige (School Superintendent, Houston, Texas; former Dean, College of Education, Texas Southern University)
Health and Human Services: Tommy G. Thompson (Wisconsin Governor, former State Assemblyman)
Interior: Gale A. Norton (Senior Counsel, Law Firm; former Colorado Attorney General, earlier service in the U.S. Departments of Interior and Agriculture)
Veterans Affairs: Anthony Principi (President, OTC Medical Services, Inc.; former Deputy Secretary and Secretary of Veterans Affairs, Chief Counsel and Staff Director, Senate Committee on Veterans Affairs)

January 2:
Energy: Spencer Abraham (former Michigan Senator and aide to Vice President Dan Quayle)
Labor: Linda Chavez (President, Center for Equal Opportunity; former Director of the U.S. Commission on Civil Rights) Chavez was replaced by Elaine Lan Chao on January 11.
Transportation: Norman Y. Mineta (Secretary of Commerce; former member House of Representatives, San Jose, California, and Mayor)

from education, and the usual number of lawyers. Much was made by Clinton of having a diverse cabinet, one that would "look like America." Transition chair Cheney stated that the Bush cabinet would be diverse but few expected that white males would actually be in the minority (as they were too among the original Clinton cabinet secretaries). The group included two Asian Americans, two African Americans, one Arab American, one Hispanic American (two originally), and four women.

RATING THE BUSH TRANSITION

President-elect Bush is often compared to President-elect Reagan, primarily in terms of a more delegating style and less attention to policy details. A comparison of their activities during the transition period, however, shows a different pattern of behavior. By design, as suited to his preferences, Reagan played very little public role during the transition. As one of his top aides explained: "Our whole idea was to build up to the inaugural as the big event of the transition, rather than having a series of small [or] major events."[36]

Reagan's autobiography does not contain the word "transition" in the index. Chapter 35 ends with the concession call from Carter; chapter 36 begins with his activities at the inauguration.[37] Reagan held a press conference after the election and then left for his ranch in California. He did not personally announce or appear with those he appointed to the cabinet. He conducted no conferences or seminars. He visited Washington twice, mostly to meet with President Carter, congressional leaders, and other officials.

By contrast, Bush personally announced all of his cabinet appointments, as well as several of the principal White House staff designations. He held publicized meetings with religious (mostly African American ministers), business and industrial, education, national security, and congressional leaders and representatives. He met with Democratic Senator John Breaux (Louisiana) to explore the possibility of his joining the new administration. His two visits to Washington were more substantive and less social than were those of Reagan.

It is true, of course, that political circumstances help to explain these differences. Reagan defeated an incumbent president by an Electoral College landslide; Bush's victory was in doubt until December 13. Congressional Republicans had impressive gains in 1980; they had a net loss of seats in both houses in 2000. But there are also important differences in the personal engagement of the two presidents with their staffs and appointees, with Bush much more interactive, if similarities in their limited command of policy details.

It was reported that Clay Johnson, the director of the Bush transition, had an extensive reading list of books and articles to aid him in preparing to do his job. His objective? "Learn the lessons of history so Bush isn't condemned to repeat it."[38] Johnson formulated several lessons based on his reading:

1. The hiring order follows the administration's policy priorities
2. Hire White House staff before agency bigwigs
3. Create a system to resist patronage
4. Have a good idea of who will staff your administration well before the election
5. Develop a clear set of goals[39]

How well did the Bush team do by these markers? In regard to the hiring order and policy priorities, it is doubtful that the order as sequence, if that is what Johnson meant, was all that important for a hiring process that took place in seventeen days. If, however, Johnson simply meant that the president-elect must appoint persons who will be enthusiastic and, even more, effective promoters of his policy priorities, then Bush receives strong marks. That is not to say that his selections will simply march to White House orders. Rather, their strength by reason of experience suggests that they will enhance the president-elect's priorities and policy preferences with their active engagement in the issues. The challenge for the president will be to guarantee this result.[40]

Johnson's second lesson—hire the White House staff first—was well applied. In fact, there never seemed to be any doubt that Bush's closest aides—Fleisher, Hughes, Joe Allbaugh, and Rove—would have important staff positions in or near the White House. They are, in fact, an extension of the president-elect, much in the manner of Kennedy's aides in 1960. In addition, however, Bush announced Card as Chief of Staff even before December 13, thus signaling who would be his organizational lead person in the White House. Rice was tapped for National Security Adviser just after Powell was announced as Secretary of State, as was Gonzalez for White House Counsel.

It is difficult to judge the extent to which the Bush team has been able to resist patronage.[41] What can be said, however, is that the delay in the official start of the transition meant that cabinet secretaries and Vother major appointments were made before transition teams were in place. The reverse is usually the case, with the result that the team members may come to expect subcabinet appointments themselves or be viewed as providing access for patronage appointments. Liaison chiefs to the major departments and agencies were designated on December 20, but by the time they were at work, most of the cabinet secretaries were already announced.[42] Accordingly, the secretary-designates could think about their own appointments independent of the transition teams.

The fourth lesson—staff in your head before the election—teaches forward thinking about who should be in an administration. What should the class picture of a presidency look like? Johnson stated: "We had done a good bit of thinking, a lot of networking, about the types of people we should be looking for."[43] He acknowledged that an MBA/MIT Sloan School of Management approach dominated the team's thinking about the transition. It is also apparent that in Cheney and Card, Bush had selected a Vice President and Chief of Staff with impressive experience in executive management. Neither had to be urged during the campaign to think about postelection responsibilities should their team win. Their experience was such as to make advance planning a certainty. Also contributing, perhaps, was the optimism, some said even cockiness, of Bush about his chances. He expected to be the next president.

Clay Johnson's final lesson—develop a clear set of goals—was influential during and after the transition. The supporting evidence comes from the meetings of the president-elect with various groups and in his statements reiterating his agenda from the campaign. A downturn in the stock market appeared to have increased the chances for an across-the-board tax cut. And there was evidence of cross-party support for education, prescription drugs, and defense proposals. Priority-setting and sequencing became apparent during the first month in office as the president designated an issue for each week—education, faith-based giving, tax cuts, and defense. He then took to the road in a Clinton-style campaign for tax cuts.

Overall, the Bush transition receives relatively strong interim grades by the tests of Johnson's five lessons. I identified a somewhat longer list of lessons, drawn from interviews with transition officials for four presidencies (Nixon, Carter, Reagan, and Clinton), the transition memos of Neustadt, and many of the same books relied on by Johnson.[44] Several of these lessons overlap those specified by Johnson; others merit comment.

1. Find Out How the White House Works

This lesson was primarily derivative of the Clinton transition, an experience no one wanted to repeat. Harrison Wellford, a member of Clinton's planning group, described the scene on inauguration day 1993: "Standing outside of the northwest gate was a long line of senior White House people trying to get in. But their White House passes had been screwed up. . . . People didn't understand how to park. They didn't understand how to use the telephones. The computers didn't have hard drives. The White House switchboard was in absolute chaos."[45] It was unlikely that the Bush team would experience these problems given that the new president was the son of a president, even more because there were two former White House Chiefs of Staff (Cheney and Donald H. Rumsfeld) in the Bush entourage accompanied by Card, who, as transition director for the outgoing President Bush in 1993, had a front-row seat for the chaotic Clinton entrance.

2. Fill the "Inner Cabinet" Posts Early

The standard view is that the international community should be advised as early as possible as to who will constitute the foreign policy–national security team of a new president. Bush sent strong signals prior to the confirmation of his own victory that Powell and Rice would be appointed. Treasury and Defense are also considered to be prime "inner cabinet" appointments of importance both domestically and internationally. Paul H. O'Neill was selected in an early round, Rumsfeld later due to questions about Dan Coats, whose name was first floated.

3. Let Appointments Speak for Policy

This advice essentially follows from the caveat that a president-elect is not a president. The appointments, reiteration of the agenda from the campaign, and meetings with representatives of various groups all send signals as to what to expect. But pronouncements on pending policy matters should be avoided. For the most part, the Bush team followed this advice. But Bush himself acknowledged that he may have erred in commenting on the Federal Reserve's action to cut interest rates in early January. He was criticized for his enthusiastic endorsement of this action and he "tended to agree" with the criticism.[46] Clinton White House economic aides were also critical of comments by both Cheney and Bush regarding the downturn in the economy, again illustrating the

fine line between stressing an agenda for the near future and commenting on issues still before the sitting president.

4. Separate Important Transition Tasks

Two huge tasks, unique to American politics, face transition managers—the dismantling of a campaign apparatus and the building of an
administration. They are related by reason of the people and assign-
ments involved—that is, expectant campaign workers and jobs to be
filled. In the Reagan transition, these tasks were separated to good
effect: Edwin Meese in charge of the dismantling, James Baker in charge
of building an administration. In the Bush case, the prolonged recount
and legal battles in Florida had the effect of dividing campaigning from
administration building. The unavailability of federal funds and office
space also had an effect. Many campaign staff were diverted to Florida
rather than to transition teams or task groups in Washington. They were
paid by privately raised funds, much as they were during the primary
races (only in this case by funds raised for legal challenges).

The person in charge of this diverted campaign staff apparatus was
the same James Baker, along with his former aide, Margaret Tutweiler.
Meanwhile Cheney and Card were freed to prepare the transition and
manage the advance planning for building an administration. And the
president-elect consulted both sets of operatives, relatively unimpeded
by press scrutiny, most of whom were covering the vote count in
Florida.

5. Feed the Press

A Reagan aide explained: "You have to meet the press's professional
need to produce a story." Another observed that if the new team does
not supply information, "the press is going to write all kind of crystal
balling into it."[47] There was little or no need to "feed the press" during
the Florida recount and court contests. Not even President Clinton
could get front-page coverage of his travels during this time. The two
campaigns had to respond to events essentially beyond their control as
lawyers and judges took center stage. Once Bush had won, the media
concentrated on the appointments, which were announced at a rapid
pace. Coverage that otherwise would have extended over a ten-week
period was concentrated in half of that time. The press was being fed.

SUMMARY

The Bush transition was one of the most efficient, disciplined, and effective in the modern era. Of postwar cases of party shifts, it was more like that of Kennedy and Reagan than either Carter or Clinton. The team receives high grades on nearly all of the standard tests. It also does well by the Neustadt test of anxiety to leave campaigning for governing. I think there can be little doubt that the president-elect and his advisers were pleased to substitute vote-counting on Capitol Hill for vote-counting in Florida and the courts.

Would the Bush transition have been as effective had he won on election day? Did the prolonged count in Florida contribute to a streamlined transition? There is evidence to suggest a positive response to both questions. Taking the second first, what happened surely did force an acceleration of decisions. It was unlikely that Bush would have moved as swiftly under ordinary circumstances as there would have been no reason to do so. Also, the shortened period affected the organization and impact of transition teams and seemingly reduced the pressure of patronage in the immediate term.

Surely no one would recommend repeating the 2000 experience. Yet the Bush transition may provide lessons for future presidents–elect, primarily as regards the advantages of preparation, organization, separation, and communication. The Bush team was well prepared in advance. It created an effective organization even prior to receiving government funds, campaigning and governing functions were separated, and the president-elect communicated with several groups vital to his policy priorities.

A positive response to the first question finds support in the advanced preparations by the Bush team and the high probability that then, as later, Cheney would have chaired the transition. Bush also would have had available the same set of experienced persons for cabinet appointments had he won definitively on November 7. What is less certain is whether he would have made exactly the same appointments—a Democrat in the cabinet, the same degree of diversity, the John Ashcroft appointment to satisfy the far right.

Still, several appointments had already been signaled and likely would have been confirmed: Powell, Evans, Tommy Thompson, Christine Todd Whitman, and Rice, as well as positions for his close-in campaign team—Hughes, Fleisher, Rove, and Allbaugh. In general, the evidence indicates that a full ten-week transition would have been as much "by the book" as was the five-week transition.

PROSPECTS FOR GOVERNING A
FIFTY-FIFTY POLITICAL SYSTEM

Perhaps the 2000 election was foreordained. We may have been head-ing toward such a result for some decades. Surveys reveal important shifts in voting behavior; sectionalism has changed dramatically; mass communication has undergone a revolution; campaigning is constant both for office and for policy; and split-party governments have become commonplace. Both political parties have been winning at the national level—Republicans the presidency often in the postwar period, Demo-crats the Congress. Then in 1994, the last bastion of one-party domi-nance, the House of Representatives, was won by the Republicans, making that institution as competitive as the others. Byron E. Shafer and William J. M. Claggett explain that these results are sustained in large part by the existence of two majorities, one associated with eco-nomic and welfare issues (favoring Democrats), the other with cultural and national issues (favoring Republicans).[48] Regarding split-party out-comes, Shafer has written that: "The public had not necessarily chosen 'divided government'; it merely became more comfortable with it through experience."[49]

Change has, therefore, contributed to a more competitive politics at the national level. In any one election, it is now plausible to predict either party winning any one of the three elected institutions: the presi-dency, the House, and the Senate. Each is competitive, even following a substantial win for individual incumbents in the previous election. I will leave to others the explanation of why these changes have occurred. Emphasis here is on the *working end of change*.

Two developments, in particular, aid in understanding the politics of the time: the exercise of co- and cross-partisanship, and the refinement of a campaigning style of governing. The two are related, and each is associated with the postwar trend toward competitive party institutional status. And, to replay an earlier theme, this coequality in political strength is potentially as much or more of an opportunity as an impedi-ment in lawmaking.

Competitive partisan advantage does, however, define the challenges for presidential leadership, particularly given the variations in institu-tional status of each party over time. For there have been six different patterns in party splits among the institutions since 1981: Republican president and Senate, Democratic House (1981–1987); Republican president, Democratic House and Senate (1987–1993); Democratic president, House, and Senate (1993–1995); Democratic president,

Republican House and Senate (1995–2001); Republican president, House, and fifty-fifty Senate (January–May 2001); and Republican president and House, Democratic Senate (May 2001–). Who among us could devise a single formula for governing under these six variable conditions in just twenty years?

Always a strategic option in the separated system, copartisanship thrived and matured during this time. Each party has had a sufficient institutional base to participate actively in all stages of lawmaking and implementation. Each institution has advantages but does not necessarily cede a particular function or activity solely to the other. And so competing proposals are taken seriously and compromises are effected, with leaders having to sensitize themselves to the points beyond which they will lose it all. Agreements are then typically certified by cross-party majorities. As a prime example, President Clinton and the Republican Congress were demonstrating effective and productive copartisanship prior to the Monica Lewinsky scandal, even to the point of fashioning a historic budget agreement in 1997.

Denied the party majorities in Congress that were available to Franklin D. Roosevelt or Lyndon B. Johnson, most presidents in the postwar period have had to work at building public support. They can no longer count even on their own party's congressional leaders and organization. Copartisanship may be occurring as well within the chambers and the committees. Therefore, presidents "go public," as Samuel Kernell perceptively noticed some time ago.[50] Accompanying this need for the president to take his case to the country was a revolution in the technology of communication and information accessibility.

Equally serendipitous for these developments was the election of Clinton. He perfected the campaigning style of governing, relying on what I have referred to elsewhere as "voice": "Voice features constant monitoring of the interests and concerns of ordinary Americans, sympathetic exposure of these matters in a 'family values' setting, exhortation for a community solution (typically but not always involving government), liberal use of executive orders and other presidential prerogatives that avoid congressional participation, and little deference to jurisdictional boundaries between public and private or levels of government."[51] Clinton redefined the public status of the presidency in this manner, preserving and enhancing his legitimacy after the 1994 elections and possibly preventing his removal from office following his impeachment in 1998.

And so now we observe the cardinal case of coequality in party strength and strategic positioning—a president who won a tie in quadruple overtime working with a Senate in which his party switched from a tie to minority status and a House in which his party maintained a slim 51 to 49 percent majority. No other one-party government in modern times has entered office in such precarious political circumstances. Among the unprecedented features was a historic agreement between the Senate Republicans and Democrats to share power, the ultimate structuring of copartisan politics. Initially, the two parties had an equal number of members on all committees, with Republicans serving as chairs.[52] This agreement was subsequently abrogated when Senator James Jeffords (Vermont) left the Republican Party to become an independent, voting with the Democrats for organizational purposes.

Realizing the advantages of near equal party strength requires leadership, coalition building skills, and sensitivity to and identification of positive contributions to the issue at hand. That does not suggest compromising in advance. President Bush made this point in a news conference in the early weeks of his administration. He observed that in asking about relaxing his stand on tax rate reductions, a reporter was trying to get him "to negotiate with myself."[53] Capitalizing on leeway is a consequence of the workings of the lawmaking process, not a preemptive judgment by the president prior to those workings. It is neither politically wise nor usually doable to estimate accurately what the final agreement will be.

Therefore, one should not expect a president to fashion his proposals by that method. That is not how co-, cross-, or bipartisanship works. And yet presidents, whatever their political capital, are expected to state: "Let's start here." The most logical source for a new president in specifying an agenda and priorities is what was said and promised in the campaign. The election results may affect how and whether these items will be enacted into law but not the extent to which they are the practical and reasonable basis for a legislative program. These points were made by Neustadt in his early appraisal of the Bush preparations and strategy.

> He has built up . . . the image of a shrewd, tough manager, moving strongly from the center of his party, both of its wings supporting him, to press the causes for which he campaigned; prepared, perhaps, to compromise with Democrats or allies overseas, but only and no sooner than evolving circumstances show he must—certainly not at the outset; prepared, moreover, to move fast as well as hard, as fast as he moved on appointments in the two weeks after his opponent, Al Gore, finally conceded the election.[54]

As it happened in 2000, there was unusual agreement between the two major candidates on the agenda, if not on specific proposals or priorities. Social Security and Medicare reform, tax cuts and tax reform, prescription drugs, patients' bill of rights, education, defense, trade, environment, energy, and campaign finance reform—these were among the most important topics for both Bush and Gore.[55] It was also the case that the 106th Congress worked on all of these issues, yet resolved few of them. In some cases, bills passed both houses but were then vetoed by President Clinton. In other cases, bills passed one house and not the other, or both houses but in radically different forms.[56]

Presidential-congressional relations were as troubled, 1998–2000, as at any time in recent decades. Neither side was motivated to enhance the record of the other, in strong contrast to the situation in 1996–1997. The consequence, however, was a live agenda on Capitol Hill that seemingly influenced the presidential campaign and prepared Congress to act more quickly should the new president himself be ready to lead.

The president's right of designation is substantial and vital but hardly determinative of the outcome or perhaps even the starting point. It is generally accepted that a two-house legislature lacks a formal designator and therefore relies on the president to perform this role.[57] At the same time, once a priority is set, the copartisanship fostered by a fifty-fifty party split ensures that competing proposals will be offered to those by the president. Thus, it was that as soon as the president submitted his tax plan, Democrats countered with their own, even seeking to get ahead of the president with a short-term stimulus package.

It is also the case that presidential designation of priorities and sequence may be challenged. If members of Congress have the support, they can seek to substitute their priorities for those of the president. There can be little doubt that President Bush did not prefer to have campaign finance reform debated early in the 107th Congress. But the best he and the Senate Republican leadership could do was to negotiate that the time for debate be scheduled for the last two weeks of March rather than as the lead issue for the session. Nor was the White House pleased to have the patients' bill of rights be at the top of the agenda when the Democrats took control of the Senate in late May. But the new arrangement reset the priorities.

It is because of the tentative, yet crucial, designator role and the certainty of copartisanship in regard to lawmaking itself that the president campaigns for his agenda. As noted, President Clinton perfected this style of governing, though following the Lewinsky scandal the purpose was as much for recovering personal status as it was for achieving policy goals. President Bush has adopted the campaigning style as well. By one count, he traveled nearly a third of the time during the first nine weeks

in office. He went to twenty-five states and Mexico, on the road substantially more for the same period than "his father, Mr. Clinton, Ronald Reagan or Jimmy Carter."[58] Many of these trips were to states with
senators (mostly Democrats) who had criticized his tax plan and that he
carried in the 2000 election.

It is too soon at this writing to judge the effectiveness and productiv-
ity of the fifty–fifty government of 2001–2002. What is evident is that
President Bush assembled an experienced administration and was prepared from the start to meet with group representatives and members of
Congress, to designate priorities, and to introduce legislation. Addition-
ally, and surprisingly to many, he appeared to relish campaigning for his
priorities. For its part, the 107th Congress treated the issues identified
by the president as forming a credible agenda, with adjustments made
subsequent to the switch of party control in the Senate. The narrow
margins in both chambers ensured active participation by members of
the two parties. The ultimate success of the Bush presidency will be
measured by the extent to which leadership continues to be exercised
in designating the agenda and managing the sequence, and in determining how and when to take advantage of alternative proposals in the lawmaking process.

Co- and cross-partisanship characterized the politics of presidential–
congressional relations over the summer. Progress was being made on
several contentious issues, with the prospect of legislation being enacted
on a patients' bill of rights, education, faith-based initiatives, perhaps
energy, agriculture, immigration, and trade promotion authority. As the
Congress reconvened after the August recess, attention was focused on
measures to stimulate the economy. A lively debate was expected
regarding the use of the Social Security surplus, given the "lock box"
that was designed to protect these funds. Fiscal matters being among the
most competitively partisan issues in politics, analysts were forecasting a
quarrelsome final few weeks of the first session of the 107th Congress.

The events of September 11 changed all that, even as the fifty–fifty
government remained in place. Classic bipartisanship made one of its
rare appearances in the separated system: Crisis seeks unity of leadership
and abhors division. The president's job performance ratings soared to
record heights. Congressional leaders from both parties met frequently
with the president and pledged support. The nation thus witnessed the
most striking agenda replacement in modern times. Pending issues
receded, save those directly related to acts of terrorism on September
11. The new agenda featured military preparedness, antiterrorism measures, aviation security, aid to the airlines, and economic stimulus.

I use the phrase "overlay of crisis" advisedly. Change had been dramatic. In particular, the president's political status was elevated to levels never imagined even by his own devoted staff. Yet much that was in the background had not changed and would influence what happened in the future. The separation of powers remained intact, the two parties were evenly balanced in Congress, competitive partisanship still characterized the politics of many domestic issues, elections would be held in 2002, and the state of the economy persisted as a prime issue. Policy politics beyond the pure bipartisanship of the immediate post-September terrorist attacks was unlikely to be as competitive as during the first nine months or as cooperative as during the subsequent two. The Bush Presidency would be tested by its adroitness in accommodating to further adaptations in separated system politics.

NOTES

1. Robert J. Samuelson, "The Great Political Tune-Out," *Washington Post*, 30 November 2000, A37.

2. "Forecasts of the 2000 Presidential Elections," summary presented at the Roundtable on Election Forecasting, Meeting of the American Political Science Association, Washington, D.C., August 31, 2000. Several of the forecasters wrote about why they were wrong in "Election 2000: Al Gore and George Bush's Not-So-Excellent Adventure," *PS: Political Science and Politics* 34 (March 2001): 9–48.

3. Charles O. Jones, *Passages to the Presidency: From Campaigning to Governing* (Washington, D.C.: Brookings Institution Press, 1998), 53.

4. As quoted in Jones, *Passages to the Presidency*, 83.

5. Norman J. Ornstein and Thomas E. Mann, "Conclusion: The Permanent Campaign and the Future of American Democracy," in *The Permanent Campaign and Its Future*, ed. Norman J. Ornstein and Thomas E. Mann (Washington, D.C.: American Enterprise Institute and the Brookings Institution, 2000), 219.

6. As reported in the *Washington Times*, 29 November 2000, A10.

7. As reported in the *Richmond Times-Dispatch*, 30 November 2000, A10.

8. Charles O. Jones, "Preparing to Govern in 2001: Lessons from the Clinton Presidency," in *The Permanent Campaign and Its Future*, ed. Norman J. Ornstein and Thomas E. Mann (Washington, D.C.: American Enterprise Institute and the Brookings Institution, 2000), 208.

9. Charles O. Jones, *The Speculative Imagination in Democratic Lawmaking* (Oxford: Oxford University Press, 1999).

10. To his credit, Gerald Seib recognized the opportunity Clinton gained as a result of the 1994 elections. He even spoke of the election as a "liberating experience" for the president. "Clinton Has Shot to Turn Failure into Liberation," *Wall Street Journal*, 7 December 1994, A16.

11. Charles O. Jones, *Clinton and Congress, 1993–1996: Risk, Restoration, and Reelection* (Norman: University of Oklahoma Press, 1999), 50.

12. Quoted in Charles O. Jones, *The Presidency in a Separated System* (Washington, D.C.: Brookings Institution Press, 1994), 152.

13. Robert A. Dahl, "The Myth of the Presidential Mandate," *Political Science Quarterly* 105 (Fall 1990), 365–366.

14. Richard E. Neustadt, *Presidential Power and the Modern Presidents: The Politics of Leadership from Roosevelt to Reagan* (New York: The Free Press, 1990), 248.

15. Charles O. Jones, ed., *Preparing to Be President: The Memos of Richard E. Neustadt* (Washington, D.C.: American Enterprise Institute, 2000), 147, 150–151.

16. The fifth case in 1952 also had a candidate with substantial organizational experience—General Eisenhower—who was expected to manage a smooth transition, and he did.

17. Though it should be noted that they face the special problem of creating their own presidencies without seeming to distance themselves from the administration of which they were recently a part.

18. This conclusion finds support in an extraordinary and unprecedented series of open sessions on the transition to governing sponsored by the American Enterprise Institute and the Brookings Institution (funded by the Pew Charitable Trusts). Entitled "How Would They Govern," there were early sessions on the four principal candidates: Bill Bradley, John McCain, Bush, and Gore. Once Bush and Gore were the candidates, there was one session each on how they would govern in foreign policy, a second more general session on each at the two national conventions, and one on both after their first debate.

19. See Walter Dean Burnham, "The Legacy of George Bush: Travails of an Understudy," in *The Election of 1992*, ed. Gerald M. Pomper (Chatham, N.J.: Chatham House, 1993), ch. 1.

20. Quoted in Katharine Q. Seelye and John M. Broder, "Gore Has Decided to Start Engines of His Transition," *New York Times*, 23 November 2000, A26.

21. It was also the case in 2000 that more attention was paid to the transition than ever before. Several think tanks—the American Enterprise Institute, the Brookings Institution, the Heritage Foundation, the Hoover Institution, and the Center for Excellence in Government—held conferences and published books, articles, issue papers, and reports. The Brookings Institution conducted an important study of the presidential appointment process. Journalists were encouraged to cover transition issues earlier and in greater depth. In fact, many journalists were included in the several conferences organized by think tanks.

22. Quoted in Mike Allen, "Optimistic Bush Meets with Potential Cabinet," *Washington Post*, 11 November 2000, A15.

23. Quoted in Mary Leonard, "Steps toward Unity May Point to Cabinet," *Boston Globe*, 10 November 2000, A1.

24. David S. Broder and Ceci Connolly, "Democrats Urge Gore Not to Push It Too Far," *Washington Post*, 11 November 2000, A1.

25. Jackie Calmes, "Bush, Gore Began Planning Transitions Early," *Wall Street Journal*, 15 November 2000, A28.

26. David S. Broder, "With Eye on His Endgame, Gore Seizes the Moment,"

Washington Post, 16 November 2000, A1. The details on this and other tactics during this time are recounted in Political Staff of the Washington Post, *Deadlock: The Inside Story of America's Closest Election* (New York: Public Affairs, 2001). Among other Bush advantages cited by the *Washington Post* writers were the consistency in management on site in Florida (Baker) and the separation of the lawyer teams between handling the Florida and federal courts.

27. Text reprinted in the *New York Times*, 23 November 2000, A28.

28. Edward Walsh, "Gore Asserts He Won in Florida," *Washington Post*, 30 November 2000, A1.

29. Dana Milbank, "Muted Cheers in Austin Campaign 'Limbo,'" *Washington Post*, 5 December 2000, A26.

30. Quoted in Milbank, "Muted Cheers in Austin Campaign 'Limbo.'"

31. Text in *Congressional Quarterly Weekly Report*, 16 December 2000, 2932–2933.

32. Text in *Congressional Quarterly Weekly Report*, 16 December 2000, 2930–2931.

33. Stated at a panel on the 2000 transition sponsored by the Committee on Excellence in Government, June 26, 2000.

34. Quoted in Charles Babington, "Presidential Appointment Process Questioned," *Washington Post*, 10 January 2001.

35. The data from the Brookings monitoring project are summarized in Jim VandeHei and Laurie McGinley, "Bush Team Falls behind Schedule in Its Nomination," *Wall Street Journal*, 22 March 2001.

36. Personal interview, Reagan transition aide, January 9, 1995.

37. Ronald Reagan, *An American Life: The Autobiography* (New York: Simon and Schuster, 1990).

38. Dana Milbank, "Tome for the Holidays: A Transition Reading List," *Washington Post*, 19 December 2000, A37.

39. As reported in Milbank, "Tome for the Holidays."

40. The marks during the early weeks of the new administration were mixed. Like all new presidencies, policy signals were not always well coordinated between cabinet-level appointees and the president. Powell, O'Neill, and Whitman appeared to have the most difficulty.

41. Part of the problem in an early systematic appraisal of patronage is the delay in filling all of the available positions, due in some cases to the reluctance of first choices to undergo the clearances required and in other cases to the length of those procedures (including confirmation).

42. Ben White, "Bush Administration Picks Transition Chiefs," *Washington Post*, 21 December 2000, A31.

43. Quoted in Milbank, "Tome for the Holidays."

44. In Jones, *Passages to the Presidency*, 88–93.

45. Jones, *Passages to the Presidency*, 90.

46. As reported from an interview with the president-elect. Frank Bruni and David E. Sanger, "From the Ranch, President-Elect Gazes Back and Looks to Future," *New York Times*, 14 January 2001, A1.

47. Jones, *Passages to the Presidency*, 92–93.

48. Byron E. Shafer and William J. M. Claggett, *The Two Majorities: The Issue Context of Modern American Politics* (Baltimore, Md.: Johns Hopkins University Press, 1995), esp. ch. 3.

49. Byron E. Shafer, "The Partisan Legacy: Are There Any New Democrats?" in *The Clinton Legacy*, ed. Colin Campbell and Bert A. Rockman (Chatham, N.J.: Chatham House, 1999), 29.

50. Samuel Kernell, *Going Public: New Strategies of Presidential Leadership*, 3d ed. (Washington, D.C.: Congressional Quarterly Press, 1997). The first edition was published in 1986.

51. Jones, *Passages to the Presidency*, 193.

52. For details, see Andrew Taylor, "Senate GOP to Share Power," *Congressional Quarterly Weekly Report*, 6 January 2001, 21–22.

53. News Conference, March 29, 2001.

54. Richard E. Neustadt, "Will the Real George W. Bush Stand Up?" *The Tablet*, 13 January 2001, 36.

55. A count of days spent on designated issues by each campaign showed striking similarities in time spent on education/family policy, Social Security, Medicare/prescription drugs, taxes/budget, and environment/energy issues. The only major difference was on "economic management," where Gore spent eight days, Bush just one. As reported in Gerald M. Pomper, "The Presidential Election," in *The Election of 2000: Reports and Interpretations*, ed. Gerald M. Pomper (New York: Chatham House, 2001), 145.

56. Details are provided in Mary Agnes Carey, "Parties' Ambitious Agendas Made Little Headway in 106th," *Congressional Quarterly Weekly Report*, 16 December 2000, 2883–2929.

57. Speaker Newt Gingrich (R-Georgia) tried to assume this designator role in 1995, with some limited success at first. It soon became apparent, however, that he could not sustain this function. He watched as President Clinton gradually resumed control of the agenda, even of items that Gingrich had identified as priorities.

58. As reported in Richard L. Berke, "Bush Shapes His Presidency with Sharp Eye on Father's," *New York Times*, 28 March 2001, A1.

6

The U.S. Congress in 2001:
Representation and Process

David R. Mayhew, Yale University

In the spirit of this volume, my task is to address U.S. congressional politics at the beginning of the new Bush administration and of the incoming 107th Congress in early 2001. So, placing this first Congress of the twenty-first century in the context of the past and the future, insofar as the latter can be foreseen, how does it measure up? To answer that question, I need to address two topics that are partly discrete yet partly overlapping, or at least relevant to each other.

The first is *external representation*, under which I will focus on gender, race, apportionment, and partisanship, with particular reference to the Senate. The second topic is *internal process*, defined broadly enough to include certain key elements of structure, under which I will consider how the new Congress as of early 2001 seemed to be geared toward legislative action.

DESCRIPTIVE REPRESENTATION

In recent times, analysts have given new emphasis to "descriptive representation" in discussing and appraising Congress. According to that criterion, by far the most important election in American history has been that of 1992, which produced the Democratic 103rd Congress along with the Clinton presidency. As a consequence of the 1992 election, the number of African American members of the House of Representatives jumped from twenty-five to thirty-eight (or approximately 7 percent of the total membership). Also in 1992—the so-called year of the woman—the number of women members jumped from thirty-five to forty-eight in the House (or approximately 11 percent of the membership) and from two to six in the Senate.

On the gender front, the recent election of 2000 brought an increase of only three women members to the House, raising the total to fifty-nine in January 2001—a continuation of a pattern of modest biennial increases since 1992.[1] A bit more happened in 2000 on the Senate side, where women members rose from nine to thirteen with the election victories of Maria Cantwell (D-Wash.), Hillary Clinton (D-N.Y.), and Deborah Stabenow (D-Mich.), and the postelection appointment of Jean Carnahan (D-Mo.).

These new results are not particularly surprising, but one aspect of contemporary congressional representation involving gender has received little attention and is worth noting. Women have been becoming members of Congress for some time now, including dozens before 1992 as well as since that time in the case of the House. Yet almost none of them have been becoming committee chairs.

Each of the two congressional chambers has twenty standing committees.[2] Each committee in each chamber has a chair chosen from the majority party (all forty chairs were Republicans as of January 20, 2001) and a ranking member chosen from the minority party (all forty were Democrats). That makes for eighty top-ranking positions in all. In the Congress of 1997–1998, *not one* of those eighty positions was held by a woman. In the Congress of 1999–2000, *only one* was: Nydia M. Velázquez (D-N.Y.) served as ranking member of the relatively unimportant House Small Business Committee.[3] In the new Congress of 2001, Velázquez was unique among the eighty once again.

In sharp contrast to these gender statistics is the staffing profile of African Americans, whose Democratic members have held top-ranking committee positions in the House (not the Senate) for decades. In 2001, Charles Rangel (D-N.Y.) and John Conyers (D- Mich.) ranked first in their party on, respectively, the Ways and Means Committee and the Judiciary Committee, two very important bodies. The two men were hardly new to these roles, as anyone who follows politics on television will be aware. In the previous Congress, the Democratic list had extended to William Clay (D-Mo., now retired), top-ranking on the Education and the Workforce Committee, and Julian Dixon (D-Calif., now deceased), top-ranking on the Permanent Select Committee on Intelligence.

Why haven't more of the women in Congress come to hold the top-ranking committee positions? One reason is obvious: many of the women members are relatively new, although that is true of African American members as well. It is also possible that, compared with men, women tend to enter Congress relatively late in their lives[4] which, if true, would reduce their access to top positions in an institution where length of service, to say the least, counts. Yet discussion or concern about these matters is rare. In early 2001, House Republicans *skipped over* Marge Roukema (R-N.J.) in choosing a new chair of the Banking Committee (which was, to be sure, also being reorganized at that time), even though she ranked first on that unit in seniority, and they passed up a chance to elevate Sue Kelly (R-N.Y.) to chair the Small Business Committee.[5]

Possibly more surprising is the silence among Democratic congress-women. Their party, after all, has been quick on the draw with affirmative action remedies for demographic disparities ever since the reform of Democratic procedures for nominating presidential candidates around 1970.[6] Looked at one way, the congressional "seniority system" is a "patriarchy system." If men and women politicians differ in their career patterns, the system poses a structural problem that might cry out for structural remedies. Why are we not hearing about a need for gendered-oriented affirmative action in the congressional committee system?

In the realm of "descriptive representation," the new Congress raised another point of interest. The 2000 election did not alter the number of African Americans in either House or Senate by even one member. The pattern stands at thirty-seven black members in the House (including the vacant Dixon seat in Los Angeles) and none in the Senate.[7] But consider the House versus Senate *gap*: it rose to new significance on January 6, 2000, the day of the televised counting of the electoral votes on Capitol Hill, when several African American members of the House sought a needed Senate cosigner—any senator would have sufficed—for an official move to challenge the Florida vote count but got no takers.

As with women and the committees, this event highlighted a structural feature associated with congressional representation. Roughly three dozen House districts have African American populations large enough to generate black House members, given certain assumptions about how voters behave, but no state comes anywhere near that condi-

tion. In the 1990 census, the black population of Mississippi, at 36 percent, came closest. As a result, racial representation infuses into the two
congressional chambers rather differently, and that difference was likely
driven home in a new way to at least the African American public in
January 2001. One consequence might be new force behind the drive
for statehood for the District of Columbia.[8]

PARTISAN REPRESENTATION

Beyond these "descriptive" matters, one other aspect of representation
in the new Congress is, I believe, worth taking a close look at. It
involves the two political parties, the Senate (not the House), and the
background context of the new Bush presidency. The 2000 election,
whatever else may be said about it, brought an enhanced awareness of
the Electoral College. With Florida in his column, George W. Bush
ended up carrying thirty states and Al Gore twenty (plus the District of
Columbia, which casts votes for president though not Congress).

The final electoral vote was, of course, 271 for Bush and 267 for
Gore.[9] Through an easy exercise of arithmetic, it can be seen that the
Senate sector of the Electoral College, so to speak, won the election for
Bush. In the Senate sector, where each state gets two votes, Bush won
by sixty to forty. In the House sector, where each state gets votes equal
to the number of its House members, Gore won by 224 to 211. (In the
District of Columbia sector, Gore won by three to zero.)

Obviously, a counting system that uses the fifty states as districting
units helped the Republicans in the presidential election of 2000.
Whatever the opinion cleavages may have been—rural versus metropolitan, coastal versus interior, basic values versus pressing issues, and so
on—they translated somehow into a small-states versus big-states cleavage that gave thirty states to Bush, notwithstanding Gore's nationwide
advantage of half a million popular votes.

One of Gore's best voter categories—71 percent of respondents
backed him—was "size of place: population over 500,000."[10] It is difficult for a voter in that category to inhabit a small-population state.
Probably everyone remembers the county-specific map from November 2000 with the coasts colored red for Gore yet virtually everything
between colored blue for Bush (see figure 1.1; colors represented in
shades of gray). There are a lot of states in the interior.

Beyond this, it is possible that the fifty states, taken as electoral universes, have been drifting farther apart in recent times, with the 2000

election highlighting this drift. Consider figure 6.1, which compares the election of 2000 with the presidential contest of 1988 featuring George H. W. Bush against Michael Dukakis—a convenient earlier reference point since the 1988 contest, unlike those of 1992 and 1996, lacked an incumbent presidential candidate and a large third-party vote.[11] Shown in the figure is each state's *change* in its Democratic percent of the total presidential vote between 1988 and 2000, with the states listed from top to bottom according to their Democratic percentages in 2000.

The list runs from Rhode Island at 61 percent down through Utah at 26 percent. In general, the states that were heavily Democratic in 2000 were *more Democratic* then than in 1988. The states that were heavily Republican in 2000 were *more Republican* then than in 1988. At the extremes, the Rhode Island through Utah range grew from 24 percent in 1998—those two states were at the extremes then, too—to its 35 percent in 2000. Popular votes are filtering through the state electoral universes in an interesting way.

For purposes here, the relevance of the foregoing is to the Senate as a political arena, and that relevance is twofold. First, the Senate, even more than the Electoral College, has an electoral formula that defers to the states as states. Second, a basic party cleavage among voters is likely to prevail in Senate as well as in presidential elections. Given the right kinds of ties between demographics and party allegiances, in other words, notable consequences can ensue.

The potential has always existed for a built-in electoral advantage for one party or another in the Senate, and in certain eras that potential has been realized, at least modestly. Good luck in smaller-population states gave the Republicans a leg up in the Senate in the late nineteenth century,[12] for example, and it has apparently done that again for much of the time since the late 1950s.[13] During all three Congresses of the Reagan presidency, when Republicans controlled the Senate—that is, 1981 through 1986—Republican senators represented states with slightly fewer total House districts than did Democratic senators.[14]

What is the situation in the Senate of 2001, with its ingoing fifty-fifty split between Democratic and Republican members? In a very summary statistic, the fifty Democrats represent 58 percent of the U.S. population and the fifty Republicans 42 percent. That result comes from simply assigning each senator one half of his or her state's total population, adding up each party's fifty values, and calculating the Democratic and Republican shares of the national total. Fifty-eight to forty-two seems like a considerable spread, given the fifty-fifty split in membership.

For another cut at the question, see table 6.1, which groups the fifty

? Party us surrogate for ideology ?

Democratic Percent of Total Presidental Vote in 2000 (Gore) vs. 1988 (Dukakis), by State

Bold **X** = a state's vote in 2000, small x's connect a state's vote in 2000 to its vote in 1988

```
State
RI                                                      x x x x x X 61%
MA                                                  x x x x x x x X
NY                                                  x x x x x x x x X
MD                                        x x x x x x x x x x X
CT                                      x x x x x x x x x X
HI                                                        x x X
NJ                          x x x x x x x x x x x x x X
DE                          x x x x x x x x x x x x x X
CA                                          x x x x x x x X
IL                                            x x x x x X
ME                            x x x x x x x X
MI                                x x x x x X
PA                                    x x x X
VT                                    x x x X
WA                                        X
FL                  x x x x x x x x x x x X
IA                                        X x x x x x x x x
NM                                  x x X
MN                                    X x x x x x
OR                                    X x x x
WI                                    X x x x x x
NH              x x x x x x x x x x x x X
MO                                      X x
TN                            x x x x x x X
NV                    x x x x x x x x X
OH                                  x x X
WV                                    X x x x x x x x
AZ                      x x x x x x X
AR                            x x x X
LA                              x X
VA                      x x x x x x X
GA                        x x x X
NC                            x X
AL                      x x X
CO                              X x x x
IN                    x X
KY                              X x x x
MS                      x x X
SC                    x x x X
SD                          X x x x x x x x x x x
TX                          X x x x x x x
KS                          X x x x x x x x
NE                      X x x x x x
MT                    X x x x x x x x x x x x x x x
ND                    X x x x x x x x x x x x x
AK            X x x x x x x x x x x
ID            X x x x x x x x x
WY            X x x x x x x x x x x x
UT    26% X x x x x x x x
```

Figure 6.1   Partisan Drift of the Fifty States, Comparing Votes for George H. W. Bush (1988) and George W. Bush (2000)

Table 6.1   Party Representation in the U.S. Senate (January 2001) According to Population Size of State (2000 Census)

Quintiles by Pop	No. of Dem Sens	No. of GOP Sens	Pop % of USA	No. of Cong. Districts	States Carried by Gore	Gore % of Vote	Sates in Quintile
1–10	13	7	54%	13–53	6	51	CA, TX, NY, FL, IL, PA, OH, MI, NJ, GA
11–20	11	9	22%	8–13	4	49	NC, VA, MA, IN, WA, TN, MO, WI, MD, AZ
21–30	9	11	14%	5–8	4	45	MN, LA, AL, CO, KY, SC, OK, OR, CT, IA
31–40	6	14	7%	2–4	2	41	MS, KS, AR, UT, NV, NM, WV, NE, ID, ME
41–50	11	9	3%	1–2	4	45	NH, HI, RI, MET, DE, SD, ND, AK, VT, WY

states into (five) quintiles according to their populations in the 2000 census. In the top bracket, California through Georgia, which accommodates 54 percent of the U.S. population, the Democrats now hold thirteen of twenty Senate seats. They have not always been that successful in recent times: one feature of the 1990s was that the Republicans managed to capture Senate seats in Georgia, Illinois, Michigan, Ohio (two), and Texas, and keep holding one or more in Florida, New York, Pennsylvania, and Texas.

But now the pattern has reverted to the Democratic edge of the 1980s. Since 1994, Republican-held seats in the highest-population bracket have fallen away to Charles Schumer (D-N.Y.), Bill Nelson (D-Fla.), Deborah Stabenow (D-Mich.), and Zell Miller (D-Ga.). In table 6.1, the population bracket second from the bottom, Mississippi through Maine, supplies the chief current Republican edge in Senate holdings.

In short, the present is a good-luck time for the Republicans in the Senate electoral sphere, at least in some respects. Granted, membership numbers for the two parties were an even fifty-fifty as of January 2001. In fact, considering the current relation between demographics and party, it is close to a miracle that the Democrats have been doing slightly better as of 2000–2001 in Senate holdings than they have in House holdings or the Electoral College. The GOP's luck lies in the differing constituents-per-senator statistics of the parties, however calculated.

As it happens, there is a related gender twist. Currently, women members make up 13 percent of the Senate, yet, through the same kind of calculation as produced the 58–42 spread above, the women members represent 27 percent of the nation's constituents there. Women senators tend to come from the high-population states. That could be a small-numbers illusion, yet possibly women politicians do better in large metropolitan areas. Also, the pattern seems to run deeper in at least the case of California, where the two Democratic women senators, Barbara Boxer and Dianne Feinstein, are currently backed up by sixteen women House members. Those sixteen make up 27 percent of all women in the House, whereas California contributes only 12 percent of the total membership of the House.

In the realm of the Senate and party representation, there is one more wrinkle. As the new Bush administration faced the Senate in January 2001, how many of its members were from states that Bush carried himself in November 2000? The answer has to be sixty, since he carried thirty states. That disparity of ten plays a role in table 6.2, which shows which members of the current Senate represent "wrong" states—that is, ones carried by the presidential candidate of the opposite party in November 2000. Thus, Republican Lincoln Chafee of Rhode Island is from a "wrong" state, as is Democrat Ben Nelson of Nebraska. As of January 2001, twenty Democratic and ten Republican senators were from "wrong" states.[15] Eleven Democrats and three Republicans were from states carried by the opposite presidential candidate by more than ten percentage points.

Are these patterns politically important? Well, probably yes. They are further evidence of Republican good luck in the current Senate sphere. The twenty wrong-state Democratic senators—particularly the eleven of them wrong at above the 10 percent level—probably soften up the Senate a bit for Bush. Even though they are Democrats, and even leaving aside any personal electoral calculations, they will consider it natural and appropriate to cater, at least to some degree, to constituencies of a type that were conservative enough to favor Bush in the election. Most of these senators are accustomed to doing exactly that sort of thing.

Then there are the personal electoral calculations. A district's or state's voting cleavage in a close presidential contest—as opposed to a personality-driven landslide—may be the best available guide to its basic

Table 6.2   Senators Serving "Wrong" States (January 2001) According to the Standard of the Gore-Bush Vote in November 2000

Democratic Senators from States Carried by Bush		Republican Senators from States Carried by Gore	
Bush % Margin	Senator	Gore % Margin	Senator
30	Nelson (NE)	29	Chafee (RI)
28	Conrad (ND)	12	Fitzgerald (IL)
28	Dorgan (ND)	10	Jeffords (VT)
25	Baucus (MT)	5	Collins (ME)
22	Daschle (SD)	5	Snowe (ME)
22	Johnson (SD)	5	Santorum (PA)
16	Bayh (IN)	5	Specter (PA)
16	Hollings (SC)	1	Grassley (IA)
13	Edwards (NC)	0	Domenici (NM)
12	Cleland (GA)	0	Smith (OR)
12	Miller (GA)		
8	Breaux (LA)		
8	Landrieu (LA)		
6	Byrd (WV)		
6	Rockefeller (WV)		
5	Lincoln (AR)		
4	Reid (NV)		
3	Carnahan (MO)		
0	Graham (FL)		
0	Nelson (FL)		

partisan or ideological flavoring. A smart politician aiming at future elections will take notice of such signals and possibly craft personal issue stances accordingly. New home-state *trends* in presidential voting may be particularly relevant signals—for example, in the case of the 2000 election, the surprising lurch of West Virginia toward the Republican side or the best Republican showing in Montana since 1920.

These considerations are no mystery to political activists, and some were directly applied in early 2001. Aiding the Bush administration's plan for a $1.6 trillion tax cut, the Republican Leadership Council ran thirty-second television advertisements in Montana and North Dakota "pressing Mr. Baucus and Mr. Conrad [both Democratic members of the Senate Finance Committee] to support Mr. Bush's plan—and reminding them of Mr. Bush's lopsided victories."[16] Bush himself toured Arkansas, Florida, Louisiana, Nebraska, North Dakota, and South Dakota selling the tax cut.[17] According to one report: "A White

House official said one of the main purposes of the trip to the Dakotas was to try to sway Sen. Tim Johnson (D-S.D.), who was elected to his first term with just 51 percent of the vote and faces re-election next year. Bush won both Dakotas by 60 percent in November."[18]

Also, aiming to ward off votes or at least filibuster commitments against Bush's nominee for attorney general, John Ashcroft, the Republican Majority Issues Committee ran pro-Ashcroft television ads in South Dakota and Montana targeting Democratic senators Thomas Daschle, Tim Johnson, and Max Baucus.[19] The American Conservative Union plotted pro-Ashcroft radio ads "in states with Democratic senators viewed as being on the fence, including Wisconsin [which Gore carried by only a few thousand votes], Montana, West Virginia, and North Carolina."[20] Not to be outdone, the National Abortion and Reproductive Rights Action League launched an anti-Ashcroft radio campaign to firm up a few shaky Democrats and target three Republicans from states carried by Gore (see table 6.2)—Susan Collins and Olympia Snowe of Maine and Arlen Specter of Pennsylvania.[21]

My point here, however, is that the first column of table 6.2 offers a richer target environment of cross-pressured Democrats than does the second column of cross-pressured Republicans. According to this logic, if Gore had won Florida and thus the presidency, he would not have encountered a fifty-fifty Senate as likely to soften up to his causes. In his case, a hardened-up Senate would have been a better bet. Again, due to the districting system (i.e., the states) and to the demographics, we see a kind of Republican advantage in the resulting politics.

In this respect, how does the Senate pattern after the 2000 election compare with other photo-finish aftermaths? See table 6.3, which presents data for the Senates in existence just after the four closest presidential elections, in popular-vote terms, since World War II. Those are John F. Kennedy's first Senate in 1961–1962, Richard M. Nixon's first Senate in 1969–1970, Jimmy Carter's first Senate in 1977–1978, and now George W. Bush's first Senate in 2001–2002.

An obvious difference emerges between the parties. The two Democratic presidents, Kennedy and Carter, enjoyed large party advantages in their parties' actual Senate holdings—64–36 and 61–38–13. Yet in both cases those advantages were probably partly countered in practice by adverse "wrong"-state considerations. Kennedy, on the one hand, had to face twenty-nine Democratic senators from states carried by Nixon in his losing 1960 run. George W. Bush's situation, on the other hand, resembles Nixon's in 1969–1970 (although Bush's Senate in January 2001 did have fifty Republicans, not as in Nixon's case forty-three).

Table 6.3   Party Lineups in the Senate after the Four Closest Presidential Elections of Recent Decades

	Narrow Democratic Wins		Narrow Republican Wins	
	Kennedy 1960	*Carter 1976*	*Nixon 1968*	*Bush 2000*
President's Margin in Popular Vote	+0.2%	+2.1%	+0.7%	−0.5%
Number of States Carried by Winning, Losing, and third-Party Candidates	23-26-1[1]	23-27	32-13-5[2]	30-20
Number of Senators from the President's Party, the Other Party, and Neither Major Party	64-36	61-37-1[3]	43-57	50-50
Number of "Wrong"-Party Senators form states Carried by Winning, Losing, and third-Party Presidential Candidates	13-29-2[4]	12-28	31-10-10[5]	20-10
Number of "Wrong"-Party Senators "Wrong" by over 10%, from States Carried by Winning, Losing, and Third-Party Presidential Candidates	1-7	5-9	15-1-8[6]	11-3

1. Mississippi voted for independent presidential electors.
2. George Wallace carred Alabama, Arkansas, Georgia, Louisiana, and Mississippi.
3. Harry Byrd Jr. (Ind.-Va.)
4. The two Democratic senators from Mississippi.
5. The ten Democratic senators from the southern states carried by Wallace.
6. The senators from all the states carried by Wallace except Arkansas.

That is, Bush is profiting from the "wrong"-state logic, as did Nixon in 1969. Even if the extreme states did drift farther apart in November 2000, as figure 6.1 suggests, we see in table 6.3 some snapshots that suggest long-term constancy. The "wrong"-state logic has probably been favoring Republican presidents in the Senate for some time.

INTERNAL PROCESS

On January 20, 2001, the Republicans simultaneously controlled the presidency and both houses of Congress for the first time in nearly half a century. It goes without saying that that control was unusually clouded and thin—an asterisked presidential win, a narrow 221–212 edge in the House, and a 50–50 tie breakable by the Republican vice president in the Senate. Subsequent events in the Senate would make it clear just how clouded this total picture was.

Yet an asterisked presidential win, taken by itself, does not necessarily lead to legislative gridlock. In 1889, the Republicans under the comparably vote-challenged Benjamin Harrison mounted the most successful legislative drive between Reconstruction and the Progressive era.[22] Enacted were the McKinley Tariff, the Sherman Antitrust Act, the Sherman Silver Purchase Act, a major expansion of the navy, and an expansion of Civil War pensions broad enough to help stir discussion recently about a late nineteenth-century American "welfare state."[23] This legislative drive was assisted by the so-called Reed rules promulgated by the Republicans in 1890 to allow quick majority action in the House.

So process can obviously make a difference. As of early 2001, how did congressional processes seem to bear on legislative opportunities under George W. Bush? Rather favorably, so far as one could tell. Considering that context of clouded and thin party control, the system seemed to be about as well greased for legislative action as the Republicans might have hoped.

Relevant on the House side was the evolution of the committee system and party leadership since the Republican takeover after the 1994 midterm election. Under Newt Gingrich in the winter of 1994–1995, the party forged an extremely strong leadership structure and whipped the committees into line to serve party purposes. Seniority norms were broken to elevate certain particularly effective members into key committee slots, notably Bob Livingston (R-La.) as chair of the Ways and Means Committee. Task forces appointed by the Speaker helped pace the committees. The results—Gingrich's Contract with America and omnibus budget drive in 1995—are probably the leading instance in American history of a congressional party enacting a legislative program, at least through one house, under its own steam.[24]

Yet these enterprises largely failed—victims of Senate lukewarmness, White House vetoes, or public hostility—and the proactive Republican leadership structure of the House accordingly receded. The event-rich House history of the late 1990s, offering among other things a failed coup against Gingrich, Gingrich's later resignation from the Speakership, Livingston's backing away from the Speakership after he agreed to take it, and an extreme contrast in style between Gingrich and the soothing and media-shy Dennis Hastert, who did take the job in 1999, is enough to demolish most general theories of congressional leadership.

In general, the House Republicans switched from offensive to defensive after 1996. That is, they gave up on ambitious programmatic activity of their own in favor of all-out opposition to the Clinton presidency, notably in the impeachment campaign of 1998–1999. In this context, the hard-line conservative Republican Whip, Tom DeLay of Texas, swung into place as the most influential leader of the party in the House.

Yet Hastert did come into his own as Speaker through arranging issue stances, albeit largely defensive ones, for the House Republican Party during the 2000 campaign[25] and, more to the point here, through helping set the stage for House legislative action under the Bush presidency. These functional needs favored Hastert over DeLay.[26] In effect, the question after the election became: Could the chamber's processes be rendered as propitious for Bush in 2001 as they had been for Gingrich in 1995?

The committee system posed special problems. January 2001 was payoff time for a reform initiated by the Republicans at their ideological high tide in January 1995, establishing a six-year term-limit for committee chairs. Would this rule be enforced? Would chairs such as Henry J. Hyde of the Judiciary Committee really have to go? In a decision climate of unusual volatility and contentiousness as the new Congress approached, what would be the criteria for selecting committee chairs, and who would they be?[27]

In the event, the party stuck by its six-year limit,[28] thereby going a long way toward institutionalizing this major break from twentieth-century congressional practice. Six-year leases rather than lifetime property rights is the new Republican norm.

The new system is turning out to have several interesting features. It certainly does bring in fresh blood: no fewer than fifteen of the House Republican committee chairs in the 107th Congress are new at their jobs.[29] Contrary to some hopes, it favors interest groups. In a now-stylized routine, contestants for the top committee slots raise hundreds of thousands of dollars in campaign money from committee-relevant donors and then distribute much of it to their colleagues—thus "tilting the competition for chairmanships to members who can raise the most money for other rank-and-file members."[30]

Most important for my purposes here, the six-year system with its chronic vacancies offers occasion for, although it does not guarantee, selection according to talent. Partly courtesy of Hastert, talent seems to have been a major criterion in selecting new chairs for the 107th Congress—notably Bill Thomas over the more senior Phil Crane to head the Ways and Means Committee.[31] In addition, W. J. "Billy" Tauzin brings unusual drive and panache to the helm of the Commerce Committee.[32]

Talent in these roles is not a minor consideration. With leaders like Thomas and Tauzin—as with Livingston back in 1995–1996— committees can amount to a good deal more than locations where positions are taken, information is sought, or interests are served. They can be effective production units, something like firms. This was evidenced in Thomas's surprisingly quick packaging and ushering through the House of a major tax-cut bill serving Bush's interests in early March 2001.[33] All in all, in process terms, discounting for its smaller Republican majority, the House does seem to have been as well geared up for Bush in 2001 as it had been for Gingrich in 1995.

Process in the Senate is a different matter. Facing the Republicans there in early 2001 was not only their vanishingly thin majority, but also the chamber's well-known shortfall of majority rule. New hazards had appeared in that line in the 1980s and 1990s. In a surprising innovation, Senate minority parties with forty-one or more mobilizable members had taken to using the three-fifths cloture rule routinely to block majority party moves. The sixty votes needed to cut off debate had come to rival the fifty-one votes needed to carry a motion.

This was not the only impediment to legislative action during the 1990s. Bill Clinton's health care plan in 1993–1994, for example, never commanded 218 votes on the House floor. But party filibusters, or the threat of them, had blocked in the Senate such initiatives as Clinton's economic stimulus plan in 1993 and the Democrats' "striker replacement" measure (outlawing scab labor in strikes) in 1994. In addition, the custom of individual senators using "holds" to slow up appointments or bills had proliferated during the 1990s. In this environment of obstruction, partisan bitterness had escalated, and the Republicans under Majority Leader Trent Lott experimented with procedural bars of a kind more familiar in the House to the rights of the minority party to make motions. As the 1990s ended, minority obstruction, the reactions to it, and mounting partisanship had slowed the Senate to a crawl.

This was not a promising background for legislative or any other kind of Senate action in 2001, particularly with the new fifty-fifty party split. Yet in another surprise, in the winter of 2000–2001, the Senate parties hit on "power-sharing" as a procedural formula for the new Congress.[34] The key ingredients were equal party membership and staffing on all

Senate committees plus a license to either party to bring a tied committee result to the floor. Cumbersome as this arrangement might be, it is hard to see it as anything but good news for the Bush administration or any other hopeful progenitor of legislation.

For one thing, the plan promised to dampen the partisanship of the 1990s. Both parties could engage in possibly consequential legislative work. For either party, obstruction of a go-to-the-wall sort might fall away as either a functional need or a publicly credible option. For another thing, the central procedure of power-sharing appeared to be exactly pro-action rather than, as with the Senate's jumble of procedures in the 1990s, pro-inaction. Items of whatever origin could be propelled to the Senate floor. Power-sharing is a tricky arrangement, and as of early 2001 it was not easy to see how it would play out. Moreover, it faced an abrupt demise in the event of a lapse through death or resignation from the Senate's fifty-fifty party split. Yet it supplied an early favorable environment for the Bush administration.

The Senate, not the streamlined House, posed the chief obstacle to Republican plans during 2001–2002, yet in early 2001 the "softened up" Senate I discussed earlier under the rubric of representation was already making an appearance. A Clinton regulation on ergonomics in the workplace was repealed by 56–44 with all six Democratic defectors representing states carried by Bush.[35] Ashcroft was confirmed as attorney general by 58–42 with six of the eight Democratic defectors representing Bush states.[36] Of particular relevance to this chapter, the Ashcroft case exhibits a likely relationship between process and representative base. Forty-two Democrats voted against Ashcroft, yet so far as we know, notwithstanding rumbles from Senator Edward Kennedy (D-Mass.) and others,[37] forty-one Democrats were not available to filibuster against his nomination. That lack of forty-one filibusterers seems to have been the basic controlling fact.

If faced by a nonsupportive home-state public, it is often easier for a senator to vote against something than to filibuster against it for two reasons. On balance, filibustering is seen as a less legitimate tactic than just voting no, and it is likelier to be noticed than just voting no. Also, to vote no yet stop short of filibustering is to have it both ways, which can be politically profitable. It was understandably hard to enlist Democratic senators from, say, the upper plains states to filibuster against Ashcroft, and that cross-pressured aspect of the "softened-up" Senate of 2001–2002 remained in waiting as the Bush administration pursued its legislative program. As of early 2001, things were going well for it.[38]

POSTSCRIPT: A QUICK SHIFT
IN PARTISAN BALANCE

As the real world turned, the close partisan balance and attempts at power sharing in the 107th Congress received a major shock in very short order, one requiring a postscript to any analysis of those phenomena. The shock was a shift by Senator James Jeffords (R.-Vt.) to partisan independence and his willingness to vote with the Democrats to (re)organize the Senate. That story may have gotten more attention than its ultimate consequence will merit, but it was a shift with real consequences, and the story was certainly major enough to require some comment.

In general, things continued to go well for the Bush administration through its first hundred days. On May 23, the Senate approved "a sweeping tax-cut bill . . . with all the main elements President Bush proposed."[39] Those elements included a total, eleven-year revenue cut of $1.35 trillion—somewhat less than Bush had originally requested but still far beyond the aspirations of the median Democratic senator—as well as rate cuts in all brackets including the highest ones, relief from the so-called marriage penalty, and repeal of the long-established estate tax. The House and the White House quickly ratified this largest tax-cut package since Reagan's in 1981.

Senate approval had been by 62–38, with all fifty Republicans (including Jeffords, still serving as a member of that party) joining twelve Democrats in the majority. Voting yes were nine of the twenty Democrats from "Bush states": Blanche Lincoln of Arkansas, Zell Miller and Max Cleland of Georgia, John Breaux and Mary Landrieu of Louisiana, Jean Carnahan of Missouri, Max Baucus of Montana, Ben Nelson of Nebraska, and Tim Johnson of South Dakota. By contrast, only three of the thirty Democrats from "Gore states" voted yes: Dianne Feinstein of California, Robert Torricelli of New Jersey, and Herbert Kohl of Wisconsin. That is a disparity of 45 percent versus 10 percent.

At the committee stage in the Senate, the key packagers of the Republican-flavored measure were Senator Baucus and Senator Charles Grassley of Iowa, respectively top Democrat and top Republican on the Finance Committee. They cut a dramatic deal that also accommodated Democratic senators Breaux, Lincoln, and Torricelli to produce a 14–6 favorable outcome on the committee. For Baucus, this party heresy did come at a cost: "Rarely has a high-ranking senator provoked more displeasure from his own party colleagues."[40]

Yet there was also benefit for the senator. A Mason–Dixon poll showed that 61 percent of Montanans supported Bush's full $1.6 trillion tax cut, and 57 percent said the issue would be an important factor in how they voted.[41] Baucus faces reelection in November 2002. In July 2001, it was reported that the senator had "managed to score important points in his conservative state by helping Bush broker the biggest tax cut in 20 years."[42] Senator Baucus thus becomes Exhibit A for the idea that the electoral map "softened up" the Senate for President Bush in early 2001.

That was early 2001. In late May 2001 came the Jeffords bombshell. The unhappily affiliated Vermont liberal switched sides, opting to vote with the Democrats to organize the Senate.[43] By a margin of 51–49, the Democrats took over from the Republicans as the majority party. This shift in Senate party control was only the eleventh since 1900, and the first since at least that time to occur between biennial elections—as opposed to being directly caused by them. The national government as a whole, after its four-month spell of unified party control, reverted to its now-familiar, even normal, condition of divided control instead. That had been the pattern during eighteen of the preceding twenty years. According to one survey in May 2001, the public was pleased to have it back.[44]

Much was made of the surprising shift in party control levered by Jeffords, but did it really portend a major shift in lawmaking results? That was in doubt as of early July 2001. The *membership* of the Senate, of course, remained exactly the same. On an issue tugging "Bush state" senators to the Republican side, such as the tax cut, a Republican-centered coalition including senators like Baucus and Breaux might still prevail—even in a Senate formally controlled by Democrats. Indeed, this pattern too was familiar. At the start of his administration, President Clinton had not been able to maneuver his "BTU tax" past his own party's energy-state senators in the Democratic-controlled Senate of 1993.

Likewise, in 2001, on issues where national opinion decisively favored the Democrats, it had always been in the cards that a Democrat-centered coalition might attract moderate Republicans in the Senate and prevail. Thus, following two weeks of widely acclaimed debate, the McCain–Feingold bill on campaign finance reform cleared the Senate by a vote of 59–41, on April 2, 2001, *before* the Jeffords switch. (The Democrats lost three defectors on this vote, all from "Bush states"; the Republicans lost twelve defectors, including six of their ten members from "Gore states.")[45]

Through a virtually identical dynamic, a major reform bill on patients' rights cleared the Senate by a vote of 59–36 on June 29, 2001, *after* the Jeffords defection. (The Republicans lost nine defectors on this vote, including six of their now nine members from "Gore states.")[46] In yet another model of coalition making—that is, cooperation that embraces the cores of both parties—the odds for the Bush administration's education reform, pursued in league with Senator Kennedy, were probably not affected by the Jeffords shift.

On balance, the Senate's power-sharing experience of early 2001 may have been at least as important to lawmaking as the later Jeffords shift. In spirit, power-sharing helped dampen the obstructive partisanship of the 1990s; in process, it was pro-action rather than pro-inaction. In the months while it lasted, both conservative-centered and liberal-centered coalitions managed to enact major measures on the Senate floor. As of July 2001, notwithstanding the Jeffords shift, it seemed a good bet that the Senate floor would remain reasonably open to various coalitional options, and to both sides. Power-sharing, after all, had worked rather well, and the spirit of it had probably come to be appreciated by the public. In its wake, it might be bad politics, among other things, for the Senate's majority party to try to resort to repression or for its minority party to switch to all-out obstruction.

NOTES

1. See Rosalyn Cooperman and Bruce I. Oppenheimer, "The Gender Gap in the House of Representatives," in *Congress Reconsidered*, 7th ed., ed. Lawrence C. Dodd and Bruce I. Oppenheimer (Washington, D.C.: Congressional Quarterly Press, 2001); and Julie R. Hirschfeld, "Congress of Relative Newcomers Poses Challenge to Bush, Leadership," *Congressional Quarterly Weekly*, 20 January 2001, 178–182.

2. To be more precise, one of the twenty House committees is referred to as "select" and another as "special." One of the twenty Senate committees is referred to as "permanent select." See Michael Barone and Grant Ujifusa, *The Almanac of American Politics, 2000* (Washington, D.C.: National Journal, 1999), 1789–1812.

3. See David R. Mayhew, *America's Congress: Actions in the Public Sphere, James Madison through Newt Gingrich* (New Haven, Conn.: Yale University Press, 2000), 171n.

4. That has been true in the state legislatures. See Cindy Simon Rosenthal, "Once They Get There: The Role of Gender in Legislative Careers," *Extensions: A Journal of the Carl Albert Congressional Research and Studies Center* (Spring 1995): 15–17.

5. See Juliet Eilperin, "House GOP's Chair Shuffle Begins," *Washington Post,*

14 November 2000, online; and Kathleen Day, "Bigger Chair in the House," *Washington Post*, 22 January 2001, A4.

6. See Byron E. Shafer, *Quiet Revolution: The Struggle for the Democratic Party and the Shaping of Post-Reform Politics* (New York: Russell Sage Foundation, 1983).

7. See Hirschfeld, "Congress of Relative Newcomers."

8. See Katharine Q. Seelye, "Liberals Discuss Electoral Overhaul," *New York Times*, 21 January 2001, online.

9. Actually, it was 266 for Gore since one of the three electors from the District of Columbia, which Gore carried, abstained. That elector was presumably available for Gore if needed.

10. Marjorie Connelly, "Who Voted: A Portrait of American Politics, 1976–2000," *New York Times*, 12 November 2000, online.

11. Ross Perot won 19 percent and 8 percent of the vote in 1992 and 1996, respectively. Ralph Nader's showing of 2.7 percent in 2000 was puny by comparison. There was no third-party candidate of importance in 1988.

12. Charles Stewart III and Barry R. Weingast, "Stacking the Senate, Changing the Nation: Republican Rotten Boroughs, Statehood Politics, and American Political Development," *Studies in American Political Development* 6 (1992): 223–271.

13. Frances E. Lee and Bruce I. Oppenheimer, *Sizing Up the Senate: The Unequal Consequences of Equal Representation* (Chicago: University of Chicago Press, 1999), 116–121.

14. For example, the 53 Republican senators in 1981 represented states with 418 House districts. The 46 Democratic senators that year represented states with 442 House districts. Senator Harry Byrd Jr. (Ind.-Va.) represented a state with ten House districts. These numbers total to 870, twice the size of the House membership of 435, reflecting the two-senators-per-state formula of the Senate. For a similar calculation, see Bruce I. Oppenheimer, "Split Party Control of Congress, 1981–86: Exploring Electoral and Apportionment Explanations," *American Journal of Political Science* 33 (1989): 653–669.

15. In percentage terms, that is 20 percent and 10 percent of the Senate, respectively. By contrast, the House in early 2001 had forty-six Democratic members from districts carried by Bush and forty Republican members from districts carried by Gore. That is respectively 11 percent and 9 percent of the House.

16. Eric Schmitt, "G.O.P. Tax-Cut Ads Take on Senators from Big Bush States," *New York Times*, 17 January 2001, online.

17. Frank Bruni and Alison Mitchell, "Bush Pushes Hard to Woo Democrats over to Tax Plan," *New York Times*, 5 March 2001, online; Shailagh Murray, David Rogers, and Jim VandeHei, "House Prepares to Pass Tax-Rate Cut, but Full Package Will See Long Debate," *Wall Street Journal*, 5 March 2001, online; Marc Lacey, "Bush Deploys Charm on Daschle in Pushing Tax Cut," *New York Times*, 10 March 2001, online; and Marc Lacey, "Bush Calls Tax Cut Vote a Victory for America," *New York Times*, 9 March 2001, online.

18. Mike Allen, "Senate Fight Opens in S.D.," *Washington Post*, 9 March 2001, A1.

19. David A. Vise and Dan Eggen, "Democrats, Ashcroft Duel on Racial Issues," *Washington Post*, 18 January 2001, Al; and Helen Dewar and David Vise, "Leahy to Vote against Ashcroft," *Washington Post*, 30 January 2001, A2.

20. Dan Eggen and Helen Dewar, "Ashcroft Opponents Question Veracity," *Washington Post*, 26 January 2001, A10.

21. Paul Kane, "Democrats Struggle to Get Votes to Defeat Ashcroft," *Roll Call*, 18 January 2001, 19.

22. In the Congress of 1889–1891, the Republicans enjoyed a fairly narrow seventeen-seat edge in the House and a ten-seat edge in the Senate.

23. Theda Skocpol, *Protecting Soldiers and Mothers: The Political Origins of Social Policy in the United States* (Cambridge, Mass.: Harvard University Press, 1992).

24. For a comparison with Henry Clay's legislative drives in the nineteenth century, see Mayhew, *America's Congress*, 236–239.

25. See Richard E. Cohen, "Hastert's Hidden Hand," *National Journal*, 20 January 2001, 174–177.

26. John Bresnahan, "Hastert's Power Grows As DeLay's Influence Wanes," *Roll Call*, 22 January 2001, online.

27. See Eilperin, "House GOP's Chair Shuffle Begins," A4.

28. "Republicans Vote to Retain Limit for Committee Chairmen," *New York Times*, 16 November 2000, online.

29. Ben Pershing, "Fifteen New Chairmen Now Steer House Panels," *Roll Call*, 15 January 2001, B11–B13. Hyde moved over to chair the International Relations Committee.

30. Dan Morgan and Juliet Eilperin, "A House GOP Reform Boomerangs; Term Limits for House Chairmen Boost Well-Heeled Lobbyists' Clout," *Washington Post*, 12 January 2001, A1. See also Kathleen Day, "Bigger Chair in the House: Oxley's Financial Services Committee Catches Lobbyists' Eyes," *Washington Post*, 12 January 2001, E1. Winning a new post does not halt the fund-raising, as with Bill Thomas, new chair of the Ways and Means Committee. "The California Republican is leading a drive aimed at raising $6 million this spring for the House GOP campaign committee, even as his own committee, which has broad sway over tax, trade, and health-care legislation, embarks on what is expected to be a heavy legislative session." See Greg Hitt, "Ways and Means Chief Leads Fund Drive, Recruits Lobbyists," *Wall Street Journal*, 16 February 2001, online.

31. See Shailagh Murray, "House Republicans Select Thomas As Chairman of Ways and Means," *Wall Street Journal*, 5 January 2001, online. See also Eilperin, "House GOP's Chair Shuffle Begins."

32. See Alan K. Ota, "Chairman Tauzin Charts a Bold Course for Commerce," *Congressional Quarterly Weekly*, 3 February 2001, 258–266.

33. Juliet Eilperin, "The Undoubting Thomas: With Tax Vote, Volatile Chairman of Ways and Means Passes a Test," *Washington Post*, 9 March 2001, A25.

34. See Lizette Alvarez, "Democrats Demand Power-Sharing if Senate Is Evenly Split," *New York Times*, 15 November 2000, online; Helen Dewar, "Parties to Share Power in Senate," *Washington Post*, 6 January 2001, A1; Gerald F. Seib, "Lott and Daschle Split Power-Sharing Pressure," *Wall Street Journal*, 31 January 2001; and Helen Dewar, "Senate Struggles on Power Structure," *Washington Post*, 21 February 2001, A13.

35. See Helen Dewar and Cindy Skrzycki, "House Scraps Ergonomics Regulation," *Washington Post*, 8 March 2001, A1.

36. Elizabeth A. Palmer, "Ashcroft Wins Confirmation by Narrowest Margin in Decades," *Congressional Quarterly Weekly*, 3 February 2001, 286–287.

37. Vise and Eggen, "Democrats, Ashcroft Duel on Racial Issues"; and Paul Kane, "Democrats Struggle to Get Votes to Defeat Ashcroft," *Roll Call*, 18 January 2001, 19.

38. See Adam Clymer, "Political Memo: Heady Days for G.O.P Flexing Its New Muscle," *New York Times*, 10 March 2001, online.

39. David E. Rosenbaum, "In Bipartisan Vote, Senate Approves Tax Cut," *New York Times*, 24 May 2001, online.

40. Helen Dewar, "Baucus Deal on Tax Cut Upsets Senate Democrats," *Washington Post*, 12 May 2001, A11.

41. John F. Harris and Dan Balz, "Delicate Moves Led to Tax Cut," *Washington Post*, 27 May 2001, A1. See also John Mercurio, "Taxing Time for Baucus; Bush Plan's Popularity in Montana Gives Democrat Headaches," *Roll Call*, 14 May 2001, 15, 22.

42. Shailagh Murray, "Baucus Finds His New Stature Presents Him with Fresh Peril," *Wall Street Journal*, 2 July 2001, online.

43. David Rogers, "Sen. Jeffords Officially Exits GOP, Creating an Era of 'Tripartisanship,' " *Wall Street Journal*, 25 May 2001, online.

44. Zogby survey released May 25, 2001, <http://www.zogby.com/ReadNews.dbm?ID=388>.

45. Alison Mitchell, "Campaign Finance Bill Passes in Senate, 59–41; House Foes Vow a Fight," *New York Times*, 3 April 2001, A1, A14.

46. Robert Pear, "Bill Establishing Patients' Rights Passes in Senate," *New York Times*, 30 June 2001, online.

7

Judicial Activism, 1950–2000

Martin M. Shapiro, University of California at Berkeley

In 1950, no one paid much attention to courts. Today, they often seem too much with us. The Florida Supreme Court decides who the president of the United States shall be, and then the U.S. Supreme Court decides for the other fellow, and everyone has such a good time that both of them do it all over again. Afterwards, a distinguished constitutional law scholar says the U.S. Supreme Court was so bad that the new president should not be allowed to appoint anyone to it. And that sounds good to a lot of people, because they think that if the new president can appoint, *Roe v. Wade* will be overruled and womanhood as we know it will come to an end.

While all of this is going on, the *old* president makes a flock of new Democratic administrative regulations, just as he leaves office. The uninformed might think this was a pretty futile gesture, because the new Republican president could just replace them with Republican regulations. The better informed know that while the courts acknowledge that administrative regulations are, and are supposed to be, politically inspired, once in place they are to be treated as if God made them. It will take Republicans ten times as long to unmake many of Bill Clinton's regulations as it took him to make them.

In these same weeks, down in the corner of the left-hand column of page one of a couple of days' worth of American newspapers, there would have been stories about lawsuits against gun manufacturers and how some of the gun men who had won hands down in Congress were afraid of having to shoot it out with a hundred juries. Courts do seem to be everywhere with us, and most observers, implicitly, expect them to stay there.

The U.S. Supreme Court under Chief Justice Earl Warren went off on a rights crusade unparalleled anywhere else in the world. Any interest you could not satisfy in any other kind of politics you could attain by calling it a right and getting the Supreme Court to give it to you. Or so it is said. The Constitution provides that the president can veto congressional laws. But the Court of Appeals for the District of Columbia says that only it can veto regulations made by the president's own branch of government, and does so whenever it does not like one. No other court anywhere behaves like the senior partner in the regulatory process. Or so it is said.

And what you cannot get anywhere else in American polities, not even from judges, we are told you can get from American juries, who love to punish the bad guys, particularly the corporate bad guys. This apparent surfeit of courts often appears to be distinctively a U.S. phenomenon, but surely it has its global dimensions. What has happened, where will it all end, and is the sky falling? Current talk about courts displays a bit of Chicken Little. In truth, the sky is not falling down, but a great deal has happened and along a number of dimensions. For courts, like most political institutions, are asked to do many different things for many different people. The current judicial prominence is the sum of its parts, which I will briefly survey.

CONSTITUTIONALLY BASED JUDICIAL ACTIVISM

The growth of constitutional courts and constitutional law is the most dramatic of these parts. When a handful of judges gets more votes in the legislature than the party or parties controlling it, that is big news in places that call themselves democracies. The power to veto laws is a far cry from the power to decide whether Charlie or Joe ought to get the horse. And courts were established basically to decide about Charlie, Joe, and the horse, not to veto legislation. In 1950, constitutional judicial review was pretty much limited to a few English-speaking federalisms. And in the largest of these, the United States, it was not doing very much. To be sure, it had nominally spread to a few non-English-speaking and even a couple of nonfederal spots, but that was on the tip of American bayonets.

By 2000 instead, the United States had been through the Warren

Court explosion and numerous aftershocks; Canada had a new, judicially enforced, charter of rights; and the United Kingdom, which had never bothered, appeared to be getting one. Constitutional review was to be found not only across the pond, but also across the channel. It now flourishes in many of the states of Western Europe and transnationally in the European Convention on Human Rights and the European Union. From Mongolia to Poland, it springs from the ashes of the Soviet empire. It works a fair amount in South Korea, loiters in Japan, and has been sighted in India and Taiwan. There are a few island republics where there are nearly as many constitutional judges as there are lawyers.

Constitutional review starts out with a few, apparently negative, boundary maintenance tasks. It keeps various bits and pieces of government from straying across their constitutionally stated boundaries. Constitutional courts are happiest in federalisms, preventing member states of the cartel from cheating on one another by breaking the cartel rules. They are a little less happy, but still at home, preventing the bigger government from cheating on the smaller ones. If you set up a federalism of multiple, intricately bounded power holders, there are going to be boundary disputes. A routine way to handle boundary disputes between two parties is third-party dispute resolution, that is, courts. Thus in constitutional federalisms, you get constitutional courts.

The same logic applies when you constitute a central government with "branches" between which power is separated. The French hated judicial review until they divided power between a President and a Parliament/Prime Minister. Now they review practically every proposed statute. The logic is there, but constitutional courts that police central government fences are less happy than those who police federal counterparts. It is one thing to tell one member of a club of twelve or fifty that it must obey the club rules. It is quite another to be manning the fence between two five-hundred-pound gorillas named legislature and executive, particularly when you only weigh about a hundred pounds yourself.

Besides federalism and central government division of powers, constitutional courts often police rights boundaries between government and individuals. Courts may be least happy of all doing this particular boundary-watching. In democracies, to say that a government acted unconstitutionally by encroaching on individual rights is to say that the majority has acted wrongly toward some individual or minority. A court must intervene on behalf of the smallest gorilla against the biggest one.

In Norway, for instance, the highest court has simply concluded that it will let the big one take care of the little ones.

A final role for constitutional judicial review is of a somewhat different sort. Suppose you want to have, or at least persuade others that you do have, something called "the rule of law." For a very long time, the place where rule of law was most on display, England, did not have constitutional judicial review. Indeed, from crass and uninformed perspectives, it did not even have a constitution. These days, however, constitutional judicial review seems to be a kind of revolving beacon on top of your rule-of-law tower, to show everybody, and particularly prospective foreign investors, that the tower has indeed been erected. In many places, of course, masculine problems may be anticipated.

One variant on this situation, to be found in such places as Italy and Hungary, is a desire to establish a new rule of law but to keep the old laws. Some of those old laws are very wicked, however. Thus, a new constitutional court can, over time and on a case-by-case basis, prune the old codes of these bad laws. As a result, the cakes both of legal stability and of legal goodness can be enjoyed.

Constitutional judicial review always has a certain lunatic quality. Judicial reviews of federalism often involve a dispute between Joe, a state, and Charlie, the central government, over who owns the horse of, say, determining highway routes. Why do we then let Charlie himself, or his left arm, be the "third-party" resolver of this conflict? Why should a federal court, which is part of a federal government, decide disputes between that government and one of its member state governments? Why should we designate one of the three players in the legislative–executive–judicial game to decide all the disputes in the game in which it is a player? Why should we allow one part of government to resolve disputes between that government and individuals?

The answer, of course, is that courts, unlike everybody else, are neutral and independent. And indeed, when our bluff Justice of the Peace resolves a horse dispute between our sturdy yeomen Joe and Charlie, we may have the best of British neutrality and independence. Constitutional courts, however, are not justices of the peace. They are invariably an integral part of one of the parties to the dispute.

Federalism, separation of powers, rights, and the rule of law may be the reasons for having constitutional judicial review, but once established such review may do an amazing number of other things for you—or to you. When constitutions enunciate rights, they are stating that certain interests ought to receive preference over certain other interests, the interest in speaking over the interest in personal reputation or in quietude, for example, the interest in heterodoxy over the interest in orthodoxy. In real cases, matters often come down to the interests of Protestants or Catholics, or the interests of pornographers or women.

Moreover, constitutional rights are never absolute. Government may always override a constitutional right when it has a good enough reason to do so. The government need not allow a parade through a particular neighborhood when the only way to keep the paraders alive is to machine-gun the angry neighbors. Courts of constitutional rights decide which interests shall be given how much priority under what circumstances. Therefore, rights courts can give you nearly anything that legislatures can, if you ask them the right way and they want to listen to you. Like any other politician, of course, what can be given at any given moment depends on a whole host of political conditions, opportunities, and constraints.

A comparable story can be told about federalism reviews. Federalism is a legal nonsense. It says that there shall be two sovereigns. The same ground and the same persons are to be subject to both. Sovereignty, however, is the power of the last word, the final say, the ultimate authority. By definition, you cannot have two sovereigns over one subject. What federalism courts do is to play an absurd game. In the face of a real world in which everything is connected to everything else, federalism courts construct two boxes and insist each particular thing to be governed falls in one and only one box. Then each sovereign can have his own box of things over which he has the exclusive final say.

When courts get tired of openly flouting reality, they begin to say: Well, maybe a certain thing does not fit entirely in one of the boxes, but it is mostly in one, or more in one than the other, or is in one but has a direct or substantial or only indirect or incidental effect on the other. Most important federalism decisions are about government regulation of economic matters including health, safety, the environment, and consumer protection. These decisions determine either that one sovereign gets to regulate exclusively or a lot and the other not at all or a little, or that neither gets to regulate much, or that both get to regulate a lot. Thus federalism courts are major players in the endless regulation–deregulation game.

Constitutional courts set up to facilitate transitions can also end up doing some odd things. In Eastern Europe, a lot of people wanted to leave the icy cells of Communism behind but keep the social welfare warmth, particularly against the cold winds of global markets and the International Monetary Fund (IMF). The Polish and Hungarian constitutional courts managed to find that, indeed, while the evils of Communism had been swept away, Communist welfare entitlements had not only remained, but were now constitutionally protected against those cruel enough to insist that the government pay its bills. One can think of only a few better enemies for a Hungarian than the IMF. Judicial review has prospered.

In every instance in which judges have been given powers of consti-tutional judicial review, they have ended up doing things that the peo-ple who gave them those powers could not have imagined in their wildest dreams. Yet people keep granting such powers to judges. Why? Are they just willfully ignorant of historical experience? I doubt it. Vari-ous constitutional fences around governmental power have an almost universal appeal. There is also a commonsense appeal to providing means of policing those fences, and its metaphor is the old notion of a "junkyard dog." A junkyard dog is a large fierce canine let loose to patrol a fence and bite intruders. Precisely because the dog is loose and fierce, the owner of the yard (and of the dog) also gets bitten occasion-ally and unpredictably. Yet we have got the dogs and keep buying more. And we will keep getting bitten.

Since 1950, there has also been a proliferation of international or transnational courts: the European Court of Human Rights, European Court of Justice, World Trade Organization panels, and North Ameri-can Free Trade Agreement panels. These are constitutional review courts in the sense of testing national law against another body of law treated as higher. They all appear to be relatively effective watchdogs. The European Court of Justice has also become a formidable junkyard dog, roving far beyond anywhere its original purchasers could have dreamed it would go, and gaining a great deal of support in doing so.

Currently, the most dramatic example of the appeal of courts in spite of their potential dangers is the move toward a permanent international war-crimes tribunal, set against the background of the Pinochet deci-sions by the House of Lords and the activities of the Bosnian tribunal. Enthusiasm for the robe abounds, even though our experience clearly shows us that a war-crimes court might well interfere disastrously in delicate national or international negotiations aimed at achieving a cease-fire, ending a war, or easing out a bloody dictator.

For example, it may create high incentives *against* participation in peacekeeping forces. It may make travel outside their own borders impossible for the American President and British Prime Minister. It may order invasions. If all of this seems far-fetched and a bit hysterical, we must recall just how far other higher law courts have gone. And war-crimes law is higher law with a vengeance. We are about to buy a war-crimes dog whose bite may well contribute to the starting or continuation of wars.

THE AMERICAN EMBODIMENT

The U.S. situation in 2001 is thus only one incident in the story of judicial review in constitutionally democratic states. No particular or peculiar American phenomena need be alleged. As in other places, the watchdog is loose and occasionally bites. When it does, those who are bitten are angry and want to punish the dog, but nobody much wants to dispose of it.

The Supreme Court issues a lot of decisions keeping the states in their boxes and preventing their cheating on the cartel. Because these are two-box decisions, they are often a bit silly. A few Justices have proposed doing very little in this area. The Court persists in doing a medium amount. In a very, very few cases in which the central government openly disdains the boxes and seeks to reach the most local of local behavior, the Supreme Court hesitantly intervenes. When it does, it is usually split 5-4 one way or the other. Some Justices and many scholarly commentators who are partisan Democrats urge the Court to get out of this business entirely, because even one snowflake falling in Montana ultimately touches everyone in America somehow. The current court distresses them by still reserving a snowflake or two to the states.

In the last four decades, the Supreme Court has issued just enough decisions on the national separation of powers to stay in the game. These are even sillier than its federalism decisions, because the Court has long since approved enormous delegations of congressional lawmaking power to the executive. Its occasional recent decisions thwarting tiny transfers of congressional or executive authority to some newly created governmental organ have been insignificant. Its one larger decision in the area, the legislative veto case,[1] actually further reduces congressional authority over lawmaking. Its current doctrine is thus that the boundaries between branches may be breached, but not too much.

Obviously then, the big news since 1950 is civil rights and liberties. The courts under President Franklin D. Roosevelt and then especially the Warren Court under Presidents Dwight D. Eisenhower, John F. Kennedy, and Lyndon B. Johnson were successful in transferring judicial protection of constitutional rights from Republican rights to Democratic rights. Defending Reds and Blacks—Communists and Negroes—in the 1950s, the Court got in deep trouble precisely because it was defending minority interests against clear majority counterparts. The court avoided deep injury by giving away the Reds while continuing to defend Blacks, thus splitting the coalition of anti-Reds and anti-Blacks that threatened it.[2]

Opinions vary sharply as to how successful the Court has actually been in fostering Black interests. For all the sophisticated arguments, however, it is difficult to see how the advances African Americans have made in the United States could have occurred without *Brown v. Board*. As noted earlier, the Court's attempt to protect free-speech interests, in this instance those of left-wing speakers, partially failed, but without doing much long-term damage to free speech. The Court was highly successful in writing a national code of police practice favorable to criminal suspects. It was successful in opening the floodgates of pornography. It achieved major changes in the American electoral system, transferring enormous voting power to the suburbs. Most Americans applaud these decisions. Who can be against one-person, one-vote?

In the hands of committed partisan Republican judges, the Court does less than it did a few years ago. Like the rest of Washington, it got ahead of the voters on affirmative action, but not too far ahead. Its current position is that you have to practice affirmative action sometimes, for a while, to cure the direct and obvious effects of past discrimination, and you may practice other affirmative action if you disguise it sufficiently.

By contrast, the Court's real "hot potato" has been abortion. On the one hand, the Court has succeeded in bringing relatively equal abortion opportunities to middle- and working-class women without regard to what state they live in. In that sense, it has been successful. On the other hand, its attempt to take abortion out of politics by turning it into a constitutional issue has been crashingly unsuccessful, creating the opposite result—making abortion more of a political issue and putting the Court right in the middle of abortion politics.

However important abortion may be as a moral issue, however, it is a sideshow in national public policy. Indeed, except in the area of race relations, where the extent of its accomplishments remains a debated question, constitutional review by the Supreme Court in the last fifty years has made only minor contributions to the most central policies of the federal government, such as fiscal policy, defense, welfare entitlements, the environment, and health care. And, whatever fervently partisan Democrats may say, the recent Florida fiasco is not even a sideshow, but a blip soon forgotten.

The American junkyard dog will keep biting. Much ink will be spilled over each bite and many nonbites. In general, the next few decades are likely to experience sporadic but significant interventions by the Supreme Court in public policy. At the same time, no great constitutional crusade by the judiciary looms on the immediate horizon.

ADMINISTRATIVELY BASED JUDICIAL REVIEW

Much less dramatic and publicly observable than constitutional and other "higher law" judicial review is administrative judicial review. In such review, a court examines whether an action, decision, or norm announced by an administrative or executive authority is lawful. The issue is not whether the administrative action was constitutional, but simply whether it was in accord with the regular or statutory law of the country. Whether or not they have constitutional judicial review, most modern states have this kind of review. And it has become increasingly important as the scope and volume of government administration has increased.

Most modern legislation regulating the private sector provides for large delegations of lawmaking authority from the legislature to the executive. Along with particular government decisions about how to treat a single individual in a particular situation, these secondary or subordinate or delegated rules, regulations, and orders are typically subject to judicial review, to ensure that they are in accord with the primary statutes of the legislature that authorized the administration to make them. Often too, there is an area in which administrative judicial review approaches constitutional review. Even without reference to any statutory language, an administrative review court may test administrative acts for fairness, reasonableness, justice, impartiality, good administrative practice, or, put negatively, for abuse of discretion.

Although some would claim that the French Council of State has exercised vigorous administrative judicial review at least since the time of the Third Republic, here again a half-century ago judicial activity appeared to be at a low ebb. In the United States and the United Kingdom, judicial "deference" to "administrative expertise" was simultaneously the order of the day. Western Europe was just emerging from authoritarian regimes untroubled by judicial checks. The Soviet empire featured the office of Procurator, a fierce guardian of the socialist legality of administrative acts. Many thousands of legal specialists labored in Procurators' offices producing bits of paper that no doubt still lurk in the file cabinets to which they were initially consigned.

By 2000, a lot had changed. In the United States, there had been a nuclear explosion of administrative review. Courts had announced that they were the "partners" of administrative agencies, compelling those agencies to put on record every minutia of their deliberations, forcing them to answer every question raised—and even many that had not— and then judicially checking each and every bit of agency thinking.[3] It is claimed that, with a couple of decades of time delay and at a sub-nuclear level, the same kind of explosion has occurred in the United Kingdom.[4]

Australia has clearly established new and bolder forms of administrative review. German administrative courts have experienced at least sporadically the same bolder activity. The Dutch have undertaken major reforms of their administrative courts and given them broader powers.[5] In a quasi-constitutional mode, the European Court of Justice and Court of First Instance are, at least I believe, starting down a consistently bolder path of review of administrative decisions and delegated legislation.[6]

I believe the story in the United States encapsulates what is happening in a lot of places. It no doubt also exaggerates it, but this very magnification makes observation easier. The U.S. story of cause and effect is complex, which argues for concentrating on the central cause of the explosion. In this, the country experiences an ongoing dialectic between democratic and technocratic urges. On one hand, the people should govern. On the other, those who know how to do something should do it. The people should not do brain surgery.

Because government must govern a society of increasing technical complexity, governmental administration must be increasingly technocratic if this government is to have any understanding of what it is (supposed to be) doing. Where the volume and complexity of knowledge increases, knowing what you are doing depends on greater and greater specialized expertise. Yet the more specialized the expert, the narrower his perspectives and the greater the variance of his values and aspirations from those of the generalist democratic ethos.

Modern democratic legislatures tend to deal with increasing technical complexity by delegating their lawmaking powers to technically expert, specialized administrative bodies. The problem is to employ expertise while avoiding the subjugation of the general democratic will represented by the legislature to the narrowed and fragmented perspectives of the expert administrators. In an old catch phrase, "How do we keep the experts on tap and not on top?"

One answer is judicial review. The legislature will set out the democratic will in its statutes while delegating the details of implementation to the administrative experts. The legislature will then assign judges as the guardians to ensure that the experts carry out the general will and not their own. Judges are ideal guardians for the democratic will because, like the democratic mass public, they know nothing and so share its generalist perspectives. This may appear strange because judges are, after all, legal experts. But law is not a technical expertise; it is a language. You would no more get a judge to do brain surgery than you would get a Frenchman to do brain surgery because he spoke French.

As any of them will cheerfully admit, particularly if something around the house needs repairing, judges are blissfully bereft of the knowledge of all the technologies that keep the modern world going. They are not technocrats. Indeed, by virtue of a legal education they are the ultimate laymen. Judges are thus democrats, but they are also democratic heroes, remembering that heroes are also magicians of a sort. They combine ignorance with power. For if they are authorized to transform technical questions into legal questions, they may use their legal expertise to trump technical expertise. Thus, expertise is confounded by expertise in the interest of democracy. The industrial idiot armed with the law becomes the postindustrial hero. The judge is a representative of the democratic public, in a position of power to ensure that the administrative technocrats obey the legislative democrats.

Another way to put this is that modern government encounters acute problems of transparency and participation. Indeed, in English or Russian or the street language of the World Trade Organization riots, the watchwords of the day are transparency and participation. Judicial review provides a double-edged attack on these problems. The reviewing judge can threaten to veto the product of any administrative decision-making process that has not been fully open to public observation and has not fully invited public participation. At the same time, the judge can say: "Given that I am commanded by the legislature to review your actions, you must sufficiently explain your actions to me that I can decide whether or not they were lawful." The judge-as-law-officer demands that the expert render his decision process transparent to the judge-as-layman so that the judge as both layman and law officer can participate in (uphold or veto) the decision.

American courts have carried this so far that today administration becomes a dialogue between every conceivable speaker and every other speaker exposing everything everybody is thinking about everything until exhaustion sets in. Then an administrative action is taken. Then it is challenged in court, and the whole spectacle is reenacted. And then if the judge turns thumbs down, we go back and start over. The United States is, of course, the home of the multimillion-dollar movie. The rest of the world may not want such big productions, but American movies are dangerously popular worldwide. The appeal of the judge as lay hero against the horde of technocratic cyclops is universal.

It may ultimately, however, be self-limiting, and in two ways. First, the U.S. example of hyperreview may function as a *warning* against the extremes. There is much to suggest that in the United Kingdom and in the European Union, judges want to do more but not as much more as in the United States. Second, the very demands of judges tend eventually to limit judicial intervention.

As judges demand that administrative agencies spread upon the record more and more of the data, analysis, and reasoning that they themselves have employed and that others have offered to them, those same judges get longer and longer, more and more technical records—records that they can understand less and less. They begin to become hesitant about making decisions purportedly on the basis of records observers increasingly know they cannot understand. At some point in the transparency participation upswing, the attractions of judicial deference to administrative expertise begin to reemerge.

Finally, for all but the mechanistic Marxists, one characteristic of such dialectics is that they acquire their historical ups and downs. The low point in administrative judicial review came at the time of the New Deal, Fascism, and "scientific" socialism, both western and eastern versions. There was high confidence in technocracy and, particularly in the New Deal and western socialism, in harmonizing technocracy and democracy. Then technology brought us mass murder and the very real possibility of the end of the world. And big science made us aware that experts were not neutral servants, but yet another set of interests with their hands out for government money. It was then that judicial review revived.

On the one hand, the environmental fervor that has swept the world has now relegitimated scientific expertise. The revived faith in markets has led to calls in the European Union and many of its members for a governmental legitimacy based less on elected representatives and more on government by experts guided by technical efficiency criteria. Faith in central banks is one childlike manifestation of this movement. If we have more faith in ecologists and economists, we may want less judicial supervision of experts.

On the other hand, much of the world is now, or in the next century may be, emerging from totalitarian regimes that rule through bureaucracies claiming technical expertise. For them, participation and transparency are going to remain paramount concerns. The judge as democratic watchdog against expertise is an appealing prospect. On a global basis, I suspect the answer is going to be more American-style review, but not so much as in the United States. Still, overall, administrative review is another dog that is going to bite more than it used to.

In the United States itself, a certain reaction has set in.[7] The Supreme Court has issued a number of opinions suggesting that Courts of Appeal, which do most of the administrative review, be more deferent to the agencies. There is a growing (now huge) body of academic commentary complaining about how costly and time-consuming agency rule making has become under the current (very demanding) judicial review regime. Agencies are exploring all sorts of ways of making and enforcing policies that evade judicial review. The word "deliberation" is flung about a good bit in the hope that it will somehow be useful as a weapon in reducing judicial hubris.

Over the next few decades, the basic doctrines and procedures that encourage extremely active review are not going to go away. Accordingly, there is likely to be just as much review, but the agencies are going to win more and more often. In part, this is because the agencies have learned to do an extremely good technocratic job. In part, it is because judges become more reluctant to intervene as records become more complex. In part, it is because American judges themselves are increasingly aware of the costs of American-style hyperreview.

PRIVATELY BASED JUDICIAL REVIEW

Constitutional review and administrative review quite obviously involve courts in the policy process, because both involve judicial vetoes of statutes or of other policy decisions made by government. The last fifty years, however, have also brought much complaint about what appears to be an even broader aspect of what Robert Kagan calls "adversarial legalism."[8] Can we maintain a civic and civil culture if everybody sues everybody about everything all the time?

Even in the United States, this view of a pervasively intrusive judiciary is wrongly stated, however. Economic growth means more transactions. Humans being what they are, more transactions means more disputes. More disputes mean more lawsuits. The very raison d'être of courts is the third-party resolution of disputes that two parties cannot manage to settle themselves. If we did not have more lawsuits, the courts would be failing.

The real problem of adversarial legalism is not the quantity of lawsuits but, as in its more specific manifestation in judicial review, the entanglement of judges in public policymaking. To some degree, judges who resolve disputes necessarily make law, because they purport to decide cases according to preexisting (legal) rules. Where no single legal rule is obviously the appropriate one, judges need to make one up and pretend that they have discovered it among the preexisting stock.[9] There has always been complaint when judges do this too obviously. The current apex of complaint is generated by a less systemic phenomenon, the tendency consciously to strive to make public policy by private lawsuit.

The problem is most clearly seen in the United States and, as is so often true, the worry is whether the American disease has or is about to spread. One aspect of it begins with a deliberate decision by government to shift part of the implementation or enforcement of law from itself to private actors. The terminology is "private causes of action," "private attorneys general," or "private prosecution." The English are familiar with private prosecution because English criminal prosecution began as private and only recently became primarily public. But this situation has, until very recently, appeared something of an anomaly resulting from English criminal law, initially having arisen out of personal injury or tort law. Continentals have always prided themselves on their public monopoly over prosecution.

There are, however, the same reasons to privatize prosecutions as to introduce markets into other spheres. If private persons are permitted or encouraged to bring prosecutions for violations of law, the state enlists, at little or no cost, a pervasive surveillance mechanism identifying lawbreakers. Private interests are harnessed to serve public needs. The invisible hand operates. Those legal violations that do most harm will automatically be the most prosecuted.[10]

A model for this kind of thinking is U.S. antitrust or competition or monopolies law. Violations of this law may be prosecuted by the Anti-Trust Division of the Office of Attorney General. The statute also provides, however, for private prosecution by those damaged by monopolistic behavior, with treble damages to the successful private prosecutor. Thus, the notion of "private attorneys general." American civil rights, environmental, health, safety, and consumer protection statutes of the last half century have been replete with provisions for private causes of action, that is, privately initiated lawsuits against alleged violators of regulatory statutes.

These provisions have been accompanied by statutory and judge-initiated expansions of the protections afforded to individuals by these statutes and the relaxation of "standing" rules, so that nearly anyone who can claim even the slightest indirect interest may sue for their enforcement. The public's right that laws not be violated, protected by public prosecutors, has been transposed into a myriad of private rights against unlawful treatment by others, protected by private capacity to sue. As the statutes proliferated, it did begin to seem that everybody could sue everybody, if not about everything, then certainly about a lot of things.

Of course, this private litigation had to be privately financed. A number of ways of dealing with this problem arose. Under the "American rule," each party pays his own legal costs, so that a private prosecutor who lost at least did not have to pay the costs of the winner. In a few instances, as in the antitrust law we have just looked at, the law itself might provide a special financial incentive to sue. U.S. lawyers are accustomed to contingency-fee arrangements, in which instead of (or in addition to) a fee, they receive a share of money damages awarded to their client. Thus, entrepreneurial lawyers will absorb their clients' legal costs in the hope of future profit. The private prosecutor is frequently not an individual, but a corporation or an organized interest group with adequate financial resources.

Finally, U.S. law has facilitated the "class action" lawsuit. Entrepreneurial lawyers are encouraged to identify a large number of persons who share a common although individually small injury, to summate the injuries, to sue on behalf of the whole group, and to take a hefty share of the total damages awarded. An individual who has been cheated out of $2.50 by a bank or a utility company will not sue on his or her own but will be glad, costlessly, to become part of a class of two hundred thousand such persons, put together by a lawyer who will clear three or four million dollars if the class wins.

All of this suggested something else. Residing in the background is the law of tort or personal injury. Suppose the legislature perversely refused to pass a statute protecting us from something some of us wanted to be protected from, like tobacco or cell phones or pictures of naked women or breast implants or guns. Either on our own initiative or at the behest of some gallant band of lawyers, we can get ourselves together and sue the maker of the hated item in one or a thousand courts, alleging that some of us or our deceased relatives have been personally injured by the maker's product. Sometimes we may have to discover a new injury, like the shock to our system at seeing an old tree cut down or the disesteem we encounter as beer drinkers when pictures of naked, frolicking beer drinkers appear on the Internet.

In any case, the United States has thousands of judges. Eventually, we are likely to find one who sees it our way, and once we have found one, in the glorious common law world, we have a precedent that we can peddle to persuade others. It may be that even if we cannot win at home, we can get some gullible judges in a neighboring country to buy. Canada is a good market, even if we rarely or never win; the immediate costs and the longer-term risk of losing somewhere sometimes may persuade our target to stop doing what we do not want him to do. And even if that does not happen, media coverage of the lawsuits may frighten our target's customers so badly they stop buying. This whole dynamic is assisted by the use of juries in civil cases in the United States. Juries may be more susceptible to pseudoscientific evidence of risk than are judges and may be more sympathetic to those claiming to be victims of corporate greed.

Private legal action has benefited the United States greatly, at least from certain perspectives. The U.S. Congress is notorious for enthusiastic regulatory statutes, followed by very unenthusiastic funding of their enforcement. Underfunded enforcement agencies may choose to pursue the easiest rather than the most important targets, and may bargain too much away in seeking to get voluntary compliance. Certain enforcement agencies are notoriously subject to capture by those they are supposed to be regulating. In such instances as tobacco and guns, Congress may prove to be politically incapable of doing what needs to be done, even when majorities want it done. Private lawsuits may work where administrators and legislators fail.

Of course, another way of putting this is that you may persuade judges to make public policy for you that those appropriately vested with policy authority have refused to make. Those judges (and juries) may be quite unequipped to do the data evaluation necessary to make sound policy, coordinate policies and implementation strategies, set priorities for the allocation of scare resources, or do any sort of sensible cost-benefit analysis. Lawsuits may push the targets of regulation into more secretive, entrenched, adversarial stances than they would otherwise take. They may undermine fruitful compromises reached by regulators and regulated. At their worst, they may constitute simple blackmail, blackmail in which the victims do not lose themselves but impose the losses on others. Sometimes they will persuade courts to do things to people that those courts themselves would find unlawful or unconstitutional if done by other parts of government.

It is much in dispute whether these forms of transforming legislative and administrative into judicial politics have done more harm than good in the United States. Nevertheless, they have spread, and they are likely to continue to spread for a number of reasons. One is the distrust of technocracy noted earlier. Where regulatory implementers are seen as weak, captured, or following specialized priorities that do not conform to public needs, the judge is an attractive alternative. Private suits are an agency-forcing, technology-forcing device.

Courts also have the peculiar virtue of treating adversaries as at least formally equal. Those who do not see themselves as having the resources to participate on an equal footing in legislative and administrative politics may, from their perspective, improve participation in government by participating in another part of government, the courts. Just as you lobby legislatures and administrators by providing them with information and argument, you lobby courts by lawsuit, that is, by providing them with information and argument.

Most importantly, markets do work. Even in the narrowest criminal law spheres, there has been increasing dissatisfaction with public monopolies of law enforcement. There have been notorious examples recently in Belgium and France. It might just be that a more vigorous malpractice regime might recently have prolonged some English lives. While harmonious relations between environmental regulators and the regulated in Europe are often favorably compared to the adversary legalism of the United States, environmental enthusiasts in Europe, and indeed many kinds of nongovernmental organizations in Europe, observe their U.S. counterparts with some admiration and desire to emulate. One small straw in the wind is the increasing role granted "complainants" in EU processes of law enforcement.

In the final analysis, there is so much overlap between the spheres of private legal action and constitutional and administrative judicial review that they cannot, as a practical matter, be separated. Groups that do not like what government regulators have been doing (or not doing) must view suing the regulators and suing the regulated as alternatives. Regulatory statutes more and more frequently present themselves as protecting individual rights or entitlements or interests or expectations, not simply declaring fiats of public power.

Why should the putative beneficiaries of those statutes not be able to defend their "rights" in court? Why should the government have a monopoly of defending rights that the rights-bearers are clamoring to defend for themselves? If markets are seen as an efficient means of expressing demand and setting priorities for other things, a litigation market is likely to be seen as an efficient means of protecting the interests of the beneficiaries of regulatory laws. As government has shifted from the direct command and control of socialism and central economic planning to indirect regulatory governance, such an enforcement market becomes more and more appealing.

My conclusions are simple, and like all predictions overbroad, so as to avoid easy falsification. Constitutional judicial review is still on the rise and many governments are going to be bitten fairly often, sometimes in quite unexpected places. Administrative judicial review may have peaked, indeed overpeaked in the United States, but it will increase in the rest of the democratic, rule-of-law world, although with much judicial caution and some technocratic backlash. The public monopoly of regulatory law implementation will increasingly be supplemented by private legal initiatives. Judges will make a lot of law in the twenty-first century.

NOTES

1. See *Immigration and Naturalization Service v. Chadha*, 462 U.S. 919 (1983).

2. Compare *Brown v. Board of Education*, 347 U.S. 483 (1954) and its progeny with *Dennis v. United States*, 341 U.S. 494 (1951).

3. See Martin Shapiro, *Who Guards the Guardians* (Athens: University of Georgia Press, 1988).

4. H. W. R. Wade and C. F. Forsyth, *Administrative Law*, 8th ed. (Oxford: Oxford University Press, 2000), preface.

5. See Jürgen Schwarze, ed., *Administrative Law under European Influence* (London: Sweet and Maxwell, 1996).

6. Martin Shapiro, "The Giving Reasons Requirement," University of Chicago Legal Forum (Chicago: University of Chicago Press, 1992), 179; and Hans Peter Nehl, *Principles of Administrative Procedure in EC Law* (Oxford: Hart, 1999).

7. See Peter Strauss, Tod Rakoff, Roy Schotland, and Cynthia Farina, *Gellhorn and Byse's Administrative Law*, 9th ed. (Westbury, N.Y.: Foundation, 1995).

8. Robert Kagan, "Adversarial Legalism and American Government," in *The New Politics of Public Policy*, ed. Marc Landy and Martin Levin (Baltimore, Md.: Johns Hopkins University Press, 1995).

9. Martin Shapiro, "Judges As Liars," *Harvard Law Review* 17 (1994): 155.

10. See Myriam E. Gilles, "Representational Standing: U.S. ex rel Stevens and the Future of Public Law Litigation," *California Law Review* 89 (2000): 315.

IV

AFTERWORD

8

How Divided Is America?

William Schneider, Cable News Network

Covering the election last year was in many ways the experience of a journalist's lifetime. At Cable News Network (CNN), for weeks before the election, my colleagues and the executives would take me aside and say "We know you have to be very cautious when you are on the air, talking about what's likely to happen, but," they would say, "tell me privately, what do you *think* is likely to happen?" And I said with great confidence that I thought this was going to be the first election in decades in which the night before the election, we would not know who was going to win. That is a rare experience. Really since 1968, the outcome has been clear in advance, so I thought that this was going to be fun for that reason alone. What I did not know is that a month after the election, we still would not know who was going to win.

Fortunately, while I do read the polls carefully—and sometimes even shape the content of their questions—my job is not to predict the outcome, but to interpret, to analyze. I go on the air to try and put things in context; I am an analyst, not a commentator. And at election time, I approach my job as a political analyst by asking a simple question: What do American voters want that they are not getting from the incumbent? It is a simple trick, and it usually helps to understand what is happening in any given election.

FAILINGS OF THE INCUMBENT

You can take this back to 1960 and ask the question after eight years of President Dwight Eisenhower. Then, Americans were concerned that

167

the country was slowing down, that we were losing influence and prestige to the Soviet Union and falling behind, particularly after the Soviets launched *Sputnik*, the first space satellite, in 1957. Americans were looking for a president who offered youth, dynamism, and vigor. That was John Kennedy who promised famously to "get this country moving again."

Eight years of Democrats and by 1968, the country was being torn apart by racial violence, student protests, and the war in Vietnam. Americans wanted an experienced professional who could bring order to the country, and Richard Nixon won on a promise to "bring us together."

We elected Nixon; we got Watergate. As a result of that experience, Americans desperately wanted morality in 1976. Jimmy Carter shrewdly read the national mood and promised that "I will never lie to you." To this day, Carter's reputation for honesty and integrity remains intact. But by 1980, after just four years of his term as president, people instead wanted something that they were not getting from Carter. He seemed wishy-washy, even ineffectual in the face of both foreign and domestic crises. Which is to say: in 1980, Americans yearned for strong, decisive leadership.

Enter Ronald Reagan. I do not think Reagan could have gotten elected in any year except 1980. He was too old, too right-wing, too extreme, but in 1980, in the atmosphere of the crisis under Carter, his strength of conviction, his strong sense of direction, looked very welcome to Americans. They were still nervous about voting for him, and he did not win that election until the last few days of the campaign, after his one and only debate with Jimmy Carter, when he used his actorly skills to convince people that he was not a monstrous person, despite the things he sometimes said, that he was not going to start a war or throw old people out in the snow.

The Republicans got in; the Democrats were in some measure of despair for the next twelve years. Walter Mondale was to run against Reagan on "the fairness issue" in 1984, which would have been a good issue in *1982*, when the country was in the deepest recession since the 1930s. When the economy was down, the fairness issue resonated. But by 1984, when it was "morning in America" and the economy was booming, it was hard to convince the voters that the system—or life— was unfair.

In 1988, Michael Dukakis ran famously on the competence theme, telling even his own Democratic National Convention that "[t]his election isn't about ideology, it's about competence." There might have been a demand for competence if Dukakis had been running against Reagan for a third term, because Reagan by then, in the aftermath of the Iran–Contra scandal, appeared not to know what was going on in the White House basement. But Dukakis was running against the vice president, George Bush, who had held just about every top job in Washington. Bush's "vision" might have been at issue, but his competence was not.

By 1992, on the other hand, Bush was in deep trouble. The problem was not *his* competence; he had won the Gulf War and thereby acquired major international standing. The problem was what he lacked, empathy, his seeming inability to understand what ordinary Americans were going through in the recession of the early 1990s. The president appeared out of touch, not seeming to know, in a famous vignette, even what a supermarket scanner was. Under those conditions, empathy was not his strong suit.

Empathy, however, was Bill Clinton's specialty; he felt your pain. On the other hand, Clinton had a major compensating weakness: character. Indeed, the very first thing that many Americans ever learned about Bill Clinton, in the run-up to the New Hampshire primary in January 1992 was the testimony of a certain Gennifer Flowers about one dimension of his lack of character. This was followed shortly by revelations about a letter he had written to the Draft Board trying to get out of military service in Vietnam. By election day, exit polls showed voters had evident doubts about Clinton's honesty and integrity. They just took a gamble that these would be outweighed by his ability to get the economic job done.

In that sense, American voters got what they bargained for. Clinton proved to be a president with the knowledge and skill to take some crucial steps, principally in the direction of deficit reduction, steps that would help turn the economy around. But at the same time, his character problems would ultimately create what many Americans feared could become a constitutional crisis. Bob Dole, the Republican nominee in 1996, did try to run on this emerging character issue, as "[a] better man, for a better America." That was a sensible slogan, because Americans overwhelmingly agreed that Dole was a better person than Clinton. But again, the economy was booming, the character problem had not become disabling—the Monica Lewinsky saga had not yet surfaced—and Americans were willing to take the same chance.

To take this theory forward, then, you have to ask what Americans were looking for in 2000, what they were looking for that they were not getting. And I think what voters were looking for became clear when John McCain won the New Hampshire primary—and gained a national following. The McCain challenge became the biggest single story of the 2000 campaign. Which is to say: the *candidate* who really captured the voters' imagination was not George W. Bush, and it certainly was not Al Gore. It was John McCain. He was the biggest story in the 2000 campaign, because he was the one who found the theme that resonated most clearly with American voters.

What drove the McCain phenomenon? Very simply, he was the un-Clinton. He pledged to end the power of big money and special interests in American politics. Bill Clinton broke all records in bringing big money *into* politics. McCain was famously a military hero, five and a half years as a prisoner of war. To many voters Clinton remained, and does remain, a draft dodger. But most symbolically, remember the one device, one of the cleverest devices I have ever seen in American politics, McCain's bus.

Those of you who followed the New Hampshire primary remember he had a bus that was driven all over the state. Why was it so effective? Recall the name of the bus, what he called it: the "Straight Talk Express," *straight talk express*. McCain's stock in trade was his reputation as a straight talker. By contrast, President Clinton was a charismatic speaker with an amazing ability to win his audiences over. But empathy remained his strong suit. Straight talking was not his device for winning them over.

During the election when I would go around the country, I would ask people what they thought of Bill Clinton, and typically audiences said that he was impressive, that he was brilliant, that he could give State of the Union speeches that went on for an hour and half while holding his audiences. I would often then ask these audiences a very simple question: "What is the most memorable thing that Bill Clinton has ever said?"

There was silence—it took a few minutes—and finally the audience would begin to titter and someone would predictably recite, beginning to mime the president, "I did not have sexual relations with that woman." And then if I asked them if there was anything *else* that he said that was memorable, someone would say, after another minute or so, "I did not inhale." And then I would say, "anything else?" They would think for a moment, and then sooner or later someone would come up with "It depends on what the meaning of 'is' is."

Let me point out two things. One, those are all exactly the opposite of straight talk. And two, the new edition of *Bartlett's Familiar Quotations* has just been printed, and under the name Bill Clinton there are three entries: those are the three.

What I am suggesting is that if there was a market for anything in last year's election, it was for straight talk. One of the reasons the election was so terribly close was that it was a very difficult choice, that Americans were not particularly happy to have one candidate who was not really a straight talker, in the person of Al Gore—Mr. "No Controlling Legal Authority"—and another candidate, George W. Bush with his mangled syntax—"I've always resolutely opposed bigasy all my life"—who often could not talk straight. Americans were not happy with the choice that they faced.

A SEARCH FOR THE CENTER GROUND

It was a difficult choice, then, with both parties madly trying to move to the center. Those of you who watched the Republican National Convention in Philadelphia saw the least political "political convention" that I have ever covered. It was instead a festival of good feeling. My summary view of the Republicans' attempt to remake their image was "No Newts, No Pats"—no Newt Gingrich, no Pat Robertson, and no Pat Buchanan, nothing to spoil the happy face of what was to be the new Republican Party. It exuded loving kindness; in fact, it looked like a Las Vegas revue, having almost no political speakers whatsoever, but lots of minority talent acts.

George Bush then went before the American people and did as he has always done, asking people to judge him "by what is in my heart"—which is a question that has always bothered me because all we know is what is on his record. Yet he was trying at that convention to present himself as a different kind of Republican, a kinder, gentler version of conservatism as opposed to the harsh and confrontational conservatism of the Republican past. When President Bush talks about his new image for the Republican Party, what he is really trying to put aside is the old image from the 1990s, and specifically, the three signal events that defined the Republican Party in the last decade.

The Houston Convention of 1992 was the first, when the weakened and demoralized forces of George H. W. Bush allowed the right wing to take over presentation of the Republican Party, most famously with Pat Buchanan's confrontational speech when he said "as the troops took back the streets of Los Angeles block by block, we must take back our cities, take back our culture, take back our country," a speech notable for its absence of Reagan-like optimism and expansiveness.

I think the second event was the Gingrich revolution. In one sense, of course, 1994 was a high point for Republicans, where they finally realized their wildly improbable dream of taking control of Congress after forty years in the wilderness. Yet from their success, they clearly learned the wrong lesson. The 1994 election was a negative referendum on Bill Clinton; it was not a Gingrich Republican event. Newt himself could never have been reelected if he were on a national ballot.

And the third defining event of the 1990s was the impeachment saga, which ended up destroying Gingrich, not Clinton.

George W. Bush and Dick Cheney were clean; they had nothing to do with the Houston Convention or the Gingrich revolution or, mercifully, with the impeachment episode. What they tried to do was to reach back to a more positive conservative style, Reagan conservatism not Gingrich conservatism. Bush is trying to revive the Reagan image of the party, of tolerant, compassionate, and inclusive conservatism, with a little of his father's kinder, gentler style thrown in. It is the new Republican Party as opposed to be the post-Gingrich Republican Party.

A different way to understand what they are up to is to say that there are two great oxymorons in American politics, namely, a nice conservative and a tough liberal. When Democrats find a tough liberal, they do very well; when Republicans find a nice conservative, the party wins.

Tough liberals for Democrats are in the Kennedy image, and for decades, Democrats tried to find another John Kennedy. Kennedy, and for that matter Lyndon Johnson, were both the incarnation of a tough liberal: liberal on the issues, but nobody would mess with them. If you tried to defy Johnson, you would probably wake up the next morning missing an important body part. And if you defied Kennedy, his brother would make sure that something terrible happened to you.

The image of a tough liberal remains a very potent one. It may be an oxymoron, but it occasionally exists. That is why, throughout the 1980s, the Democrats longed for Mario Cuomo to come in and save them; he too was the incarnation of a tough liberal. You did not mess with Cuomo. He was supposed to be the tough guy who would rescue the Democratic Party, except that he decided that he never really wanted to be president.

By contrast, Bill Clinton actually proved his mettle as a tough liberal in the confrontation with Congress. In doing so, he pulled off one of the neatest political tricks of modern times. When the Republican Congress would pass things, he would essentially send them the message

"I'm for this, but not that much." It was brilliant political positioning. They would pass a balanced budget; he would say "I am for a balanced budget, but I am going to veto this bill because it goes too far." Then they would move welfare reform, and he would veto it, saying "I'm for welfare reform, but not that much." Which enabled him to do something quite remarkable: he stole the Republicans' issues and stood up to them simultaneously.

The opposite is, of course, the nice conservative. George W. Bush has, I think, aspired to be one, and in pursuit of that goal he has also carried off an impressive—not quite as impressive as Clinton, but impressive—exercise in political skill, particularly in the way that he dealt with conservatism and continues to deal with conservatives. Bush's approach to conservatives is essentially to say, "I endorse your positions and I embrace your adversaries." He has actually done this repeatedly.

He can endorse social conservatism on issues of gender, saying "I do not believe in gay marriage," while at the same time becoming the first national Republican nominee to welcome explicitly the support of gay Americans in his national campaign. He firmly and explicitly opposes abortion rights, but he welcomes abortion rights supporters like Christine Todd Whitman into his administration. He opposes affirmative action, but he welcomes its supporters, and he clearly does not make it a litmus test: remember the shifting of his cabinet, with Colin Powell as Secretary of State. That is the compassionate—the nice—conservative: I endorse your positions, but I embrace your adversaries.

Quite an act, but he brings it off. It has impressed Americans that the president is in fact a nice guy, while he can simultaneously be an orthodox conservative. I think Republicans basically learned their lesson from the impeachment catastrophe, that they cannot be harsh or vindictive, which is why Bush in Philadelphia, when he talked about Clinton, said our current president embodies the potential of a generation: so many talents, so much charm, such great skill, but ultimately to what end? His tone was rueful rather than harsh.

In many ways, Al Gore tried to move his Democratic Party to the center as well. His was at least an equally difficult task, however, in having to embrace Clintonism but not Clinton. That is why a storm blew up among Democrats at the convention over a proposed fund-raiser at the Playboy mansion; this was too much the Democratic Party in the Clinton mold. More consequentially, when he picked Joe Lieberman as his vice presidential nominee, Gore was making a statement about *Clinton*. Lieberman had always been loyal to Clinton's New Democratic agenda. But he was scathingly critical of Clinton's personal behavior, which is exactly where Gore wanted to be.

THE COMING OF A CULTURAL DIVIDE

The result was two major-party nominees who wished to present themselves as centrists in the general election campaign, positioning their tickets for maximum public attraction. Yet from the other side, one of two themes prevails in most elections, regardless of careful strategic positioning. Either the electorate agrees that (1) "You've never had it so good," or the electorate concludes that (2) "It's time for a change." The 2000 election was odd because voters felt both ways. In overwhelming numbers, they said this was the best economy of their lifetime. But also in overwhelming numbers, they thought the country needed a change of leadership. Hence, the excruciating closeness of the result.

In truth, the campaign before election day did not seem especially divisive. But in the postelection ordeal, the country came closer to being torn apart. The stakes suddenly escalated and millions of voters acquired a desperate interest in making sure the wrong man did not get elected. What had seemed a casual preference turned overnight into a life-and-death struggle.

How divided is the country in its aftermath? It certainly looks divided. Al Gore won the nationwide popular vote by about half a percent, the closest outcome since 1960. But George W. Bush got elected by carrying the Electoral College 271-267, the closest electoral tally since 1876. Republicans retained a razor-thin edge in the House of Representatives. The election produced a Senate with fifty Democrats and fifty Republicans; you cannot get any closer than that. Moreover, the parties are as closely divided in the states as they are in Washington, D.C. Eighteen states have Republican-controlled legislatures; sixteen states have Democrat-controlled legislatures; and sixteen others are split.

The Clinton years thus had the effect of equalizing the strength of the two parties, and this was not some statistical accident. What President Clinton did was blur party differences on economic policy, while creating a deep division over values. Clintonism is an economic policy of the center—a "third way," between left and right. A lot of it was stolen from Republicans. And it worked. It brought the country peace, prosperity, decreasing crime rates, and declining welfare rolls. On election day, nearly two-thirds of Americans thought the *country* was headed in the right direction. So why did Al Gore not get two-thirds of the vote?

The experts with their elaborate economic models predicted that Gore would be the easy winner. The economy was doing great; President Clinton had a high job rating; "the forces" in the election appeared to be with Gore. At the same time, almost 60 percent of voters polled on election day said the *moral condition* of the country was seriously off on the wrong track. President Clinton had created a consensus on economic policy, but not on cultural values.

You can see the values split in the 2000 election map provided in chapter 1, figure 1.1. The socially conservative heartland of the country went for Bush. Gore's support came from the socially liberal coasts and the liberal upper Midwest (Minnesota, Wisconsin, Illinois, and Iowa), plus areas dominated by minorities, like African Americans in the Mississippi Delta, Hispanic Americans in south Texas and Florida, and Asian Americans in Hawaii.

Lifestyle differences had a powerful impact on the way people voted. Urban America went heavily for Gore; rural America went for Bush; suburban voters were split. Married voters went for Bush; single voters went for Gore. Regular churchgoers went for Bush; less religious voters went for Gore. Gun owners came out for Bush; no-guns meant Gore.

Why does lifestyle suddenly matter so much? Perhaps the clue lies in the fact that "lifestyle" is itself a 1960s word, and Bill Clinton was the first president to come out of the culture of the 1960s—sex, drugs, and rock 'n' roll. Clinton was a hero to African Americans, to Hollywood celebrities, and to ideological feminists not because of his centrist policies but because of his liberal values. In that sense, the 2000 election was the culmination of a thirty-years war in American politics.

In that sense, it was not unlike the aftermath of the Civil War of the 1860s. Over six hundred thousand Americans were killed in that war, and its bitter cultural divisions, North versus South, infected partisan politics for decades afterwards. Even some of their most dramatic individual products would have analogs a hundred and forty years later: President Andrew Johnson's impeachment, for example, was a direct product of these cultural hatreds.

The United States went through a different kind of civil war—an explicitly cultural war—in the 1960s. At the heart of the conflict was another real conflict, with more than fifty-seven thousand Americans killed in Vietnam. Yet it is the bitter and larger divisions created by "the sixties," liberal versus conservative rather than North versus South, that have poisoned American politics for more than thirty years. The impeachment of President Clinton was a direct product of those hatreds.

The puzzle throughout Clinton's presidency was why he was hated by so many Americans and loved by so many others in apparent contradiction of his policy program. After all, Clinton had fashioned himself a New Democrat, who led his party back to the center. I myself might have added "the era of big government is over," as he famously said in his 1996 State of the Union speech, to that list of Clinton hallmarks for *Bartlett's Familiar Quotations*.

Nevertheless, liberals were powerfully loyal to Clinton—as loyal as conservatives were to Ronald Reagan during the Iran–Contra scandal. Why? Not because of his policies. Clinton was willing to sell liberals out on welfare reform, on free trade, and on a balanced budget. Clinton was a hero to liberals because of his *values*. They were the values of the 1960s: tolerance of alternative life styles, as with "gays in the military"; a "modern" marriage, involving private peccadilloes but public support; and empathy, the quality that got him elected.

Clinton-haters, in turn, hated Clinton because they hated the 1960s, which they believe corrupted American culture with an ethic of self-indulgence. "Why do you hate Clinton so much?", I asked a Chicago-area conservative during the impeachment hearings. "His polices have not been particularly radical." "I'll tell you why I hate Clinton," the activist responded. "I hate him because he's a womanizing, Elvis-loving, non-inhaling, truth-shading, war-protesting, draft-dodging, abortion-protecting, gay-promoting, gun-hating, baby boomer. That's why." It's the values, stupid.

Impeachment and then Florida were only the latest skirmishes in America's ongoing cultural war. The preelection day campaign had been a contest over policy, and it brought Americans together. Elect either candidate, and voters knew they would get some version of social security reform, campaign finance reform, income tax cuts, prescription drug coverage, and a stronger federal role in education.

The postelection campaign was a more polarized contest. Bush appeared smug and arrogant, as his campaign talked about victory rallies and transition teams. Gore looked like a man who would do anything to get elected, as his campaign talked about ballot technicalities and legal challenges. Suddenly it was all about race and abortion rights—issues that had barely surfaced during the preelection campaign. Partisan lines hardened accordingly.

In the aftermath, George W. Bush finds himself trying to hold the Republican base on social issues while expanding his party's economic appeal. That is the same thing Ronald Reagan did successfully in the 1980s. Indeed, it is the same thing Bill Clinton did for the Democrats in the 1990s.

Clinton made the Democrats more competitive on economic issues, in the suburbs most especially, where most Americans now live. California and New Jersey, for example, are suburban states that used to be reliably Republican. But they are also coastal states whose voters do not like the easy equation between the GOP and the religious right. Clinton made it safe for tax-sensitive suburbanites to vote Democratic. In the process, he caused economic liberals like Bill Bradley and Ralph Nader to denounce Clintonism as a sellout.

At the same time, Clinton reduced the Democratic appeal in culturally conservative areas of the country, like Tennessee, Arkansas, and West Virginia, states Gore should have won. Talk to a liberal, and they will give you this analysis of the 2000 election: Gore lost because he kept his distance from Clinton. But the truth is different: Gore lost because he *could not* keep his distance from Clinton.

Gore could not have done much better with liberals and minorities. He carried California and Illinois by twelve points, New York by twenty-five. African American turnout was up in many parts of the country (like Florida), and 90 percent of it voted for Gore. The gender gap was bigger than it has ever been. Women went for Gore over Bush by eleven points.

But men went for Bush over Gore by eleven points, and that was Gore's problem. Try as he did to keep a distance from Clinton—by naming Joe Lieberman to the ticket, for instance—he was always Clinton's man. Voters who hated Clinton came out strongly against Gore. Had there been no Clinton scandals, would Gore have lost the election with all he had going for him? It seems highly unlikely. Consensus on policy, division on values: that is where the United States stands in the aftermath of the 2000 election.

Index

abortion, 11, 13, 14; Gore vs. Bush on, 12

Abraham, Spencer, 108, 109t5.1

administrative judicial review, 159–64, 163, 164; constitutional review and, 155; definition of, 155; expanded use of, 156; low point in, 158; technology and, 156, 158–59

"adversarial legalism," 159–60

AFL-CIO, 64

African Americans: Congress and, 126–28; party allegiance and, 9; presidential election (2000) and, 177

Alaska, political support in, 8

Alexander, Lamar, 60

Allbaugh, Joe, 111, 115

American Conservative Union, 134

American Enterprise Institute, transition and, 122n21

American political balance, 13

American politics: in 1960s, 21–25; conservative vs. liberal and, 172; Great Depression era and, 18–20; party motivations and, 24; reconstitution of, 17–18

Annenberg Year 2000 Rolling Cross-Section Survey (election study), 73, 87n6; debate effects and, 76–77; Democratic National Convention and, 75–76; description of, 74; Gore lead collapse and, 77; personal traits and, 77–78; Republican National Convention and, 75–76; vice presidential nomination and, 76

AntiTrust Division of the Office of Attorney General, 160–61

Arkansas, 177; political support in, 7

Ashcroft, John, 115, 134, 139; cabinet appointment to Bush administration and, 109t5.1

Asians, party allegiance and, 9

Baker, James A., 104; transition and, 114

Bartels, Larry M., 75

Baucus, Max, 134, 140, 141

Bauer, Gary, 40

Biden, Joseph, 52

bipartisanship, 43–44

Boston Globe, 52; New Hampshire poll in, 63

Boxer, Barbara, 132

Bradley, Bill, 54, 68, 177; campaign finance reform and, 64–65; Gore vs., 62–64; invisible primary and, 64–65; McCain and, 64–65; New Hampshire poll and, 63

About the Contributors

James A. Barnes is a political correspondent for *National Journal*, specializing in partisan politics. His work as one of the premier analysts of elite politics—the side of politics that is more hidden, private, and strategic, where individual actors deal with individual others—finds expression in numerous leading stories in that journal.

Michael Barone is Senior Writer at *U.S. News & World Report* and the leading analyst of changes in American society as they affect its politics. He is the long-time moving force behind *The Almanac of American Politics* and is the author of *Our Country: The Shaping of America from Roosevelt to Reagan* (1990).

Michael G. Hagen is Senior Research Associate at the Annenberg Public Policy Center, one of the Study Directors of the Annenberg Year 2000 Rolling Cross-Section Survey, and coauthor of *Race and Inequality* (1985).

Kathleen Hall Jamieson is Dean of the Annenberg School for Communication, and author of numerous books and articles including *The Interplay of Influence: News, Advertising, Politics, and the Mass Media* (1992). She is also one of the Study Directors of the Annenberg Year 2000 Rolling Cross-Section Survey.

Richard Johnston is Professor of Political Science at the University of British Columbia, a Study Director of the Annenberg Year 2000 Rolling Cross-Section Survey, and author of, among many, *Letting the People Decide: Dynamics of a Canadian Election* (1992).

Charles O. Jones is Hawkins Chair Emeritus of Political Science at the University of Wisconsin. A past president of the American Political Science Association and editor of the *American Political Science Review*, his numerous publications include, most recently, *Passages to the Presidency: From Campaigning to Governing* (1998).

David R. Mayhew is Alfred Cowles Professor of Government at Yale University and a central figure in the scholarly analysis of modern American politics. These analyses continue, most recently, with *America's Congress: Actions in the Public Sphere, James Madison through Newt Gingrich* (2000).

William Schneider is Senior Political Analyst for Cable News Network and the moving force behind "Inside Politics," a daily extended analysis of American politics. He is also a Resident Fellow at the American Enterprise Institute, as well as a regular contributor to *National Journal* and *The Los Angeles Times*.

Byron E. Shafer is Glenn B. and Cleone Orr Hawkins Chair of Political Science at the University of Wisconsin. His monographic works stretch from *Quiet Revolution: The Struggle for the Democratic Party and the Shaping of Post-reform Politics* (1983) to *The Two Majorities: The Issue Context of Modern American Politics* (with William J. M. Claggett) (1995).

Martin M. Shapiro is James W. and Isabel Coffroth Professor of Law at the University of California at Berkeley. His work has moved from a specifically American focus, as with *Law and Politics in the Supreme Court* (1964), to self-conscious comparison, as with *Who Guards the Guardians: Judicial Control of Administration* (1988).